Artful ALBUM QUILTS

APPLIQUÉ INSPIRATIONS FROM TRADITIONAL BLOCKS

JANE TOWNSWICK

Artful Album Quilts: Appliqué Inspirations from Traditional Blocks

That Patchwork Place® is an imprint of Martingale & Company™.

Martingale & Company
PO Box 118
Bothell, WA 98041-0118
www.martingale-pub.com

Credits

President • Nancy J. Martin
CEO • Daniel J. Martin
Publisher • Jane Hamada
Editorial Director • Mary V. Green
Editorial Project Manger • Tina Cook
Technical Editor • Ursula Reikes
Copy Editor • Pamela Mostek
Design and Production Manager • Stan Green
Illustrators • Robin Strobel, Laurel Strand
Cover and Text Designer • Trina Stahl
Photographer • Brent Kane

Printed in China
06 05 04 03 02 01 8 7 6 5 4 3 2 1

Library of Congress Cataloging-in-Publication Data

Townswick, Jane.
Artful album quilts : appliqué inspirations from traditional blocks / Jane Townswick.
p. cm.
ISBN 1-56477-366-3
1. Appliqué—Patterns. 2. Quilting—Patterns. 3. Album quilts. I. Title.
TT779 .T67 2001
746.46'041—dc21

2001022221

Mission Statement

We are dedicated to providing quality products and service by working together to inspire creativity and to enrich the lives we touch.

Dedication

Proverbs 3: 5–6

Acknowledgments

Many thanks to Gail Kessler and Carol Singer for allowing me to showcase their incredible workmanship in the beautiful "Pennsylvania Flower Garden" quilt on page 48 and to Seta Wehbe and Teresa Fusco for their incredible workmanship in the gorgeous "Rhapsody in Red and Black" quilt on page 52. My gratitude also goes to Benartex, Inc., for providing the glorious array of fabrics featured in "Pennsylvania Flower Garden" and "Rhapsody in Red and Black."

The creative atmosphere at the Ladyfingers Sewing Studio shop has given me the chance to meet the most wonderful group of quilters who continually challenge me to grow and develop new designs. To all of you, I am more grateful than you can imagine.

And to Ursula Reikes, my thanks and appreciation for making this a better book.

CONTENTS

Courtesy of the New York State Historical Association, Cooperstown, New York. Photo by Richard Walker.

INTRODUCTION

If you love hand appliqué, as I do, you probably also share my appreciation for album quilts made in the nineteenth century. I love looking at quilt books that present collections of beautiful appliqué quilts, whether the quilts feature simple folk art designs or more intricate Baltimore album blocks that showcase the exquisite stitching skills of their makers.

The quilt on page 6 is one of my very favorite album quilts. It is now owned by the New York State Historical Association in Cooperstown, New York. Dated 1857 and inscribed with the name Anna Putney Farrington, it contains forty-two gorgeous blocks that reflect the artistic talent of its maker. The moment I saw this quilt in the book *America's Quilts and Coverlets*, by Carleton Safford and Robert Bishop, I longed for access to the original patterns so that I could stitch every single block. Since that was not possible, I started looking for ways to create appliqué designs of my own that would be similar in style to the original ones, yet allow me to add my personal touch in terms of composition and color.

Updating and putting your own spin on vintage blocks is a lot of fun, and it's easier than you might think. It liberates you from the need for printed patterns and puts a new world of creative design possibilities at your fingertips. The first section in this book, "Updating Vintage Appliqué Designs," shows you how to use a quick-and-easy formula to enlarge an appliqué shape in a photo of a vintage album block proportionately so that it fits any size block you decide to make. You can use any size photo, which gives you the freedom to work with designs from many different sources and adapt them all to fit your quilts. It is important to remember that this process applies only to *vintage* designs that are in the public domain, *never* to today's quilts, or *any* designs that are copyrighted by the quiltmaker.

The projects in this book feature three different formats for showcasing your album blocks. "Way Beyond Baltimore!" (page 44) features all sixteen blocks in this book, set with traditional sashing strips, corner squares, and a pieced-and-appliquéd border. "Pennsylvania Flower Garden" (page 48) contains twelve album blocks in a side-by-side setting with no sashing strips and a floral swag border. "Rhapsody in Red and Black" (page 52) is a quick quilt containing nine album blocks surrounded by bold, dark sashing strips and a border that features a striped fabric and four different appliqué motifs. You can mix and match your blocks in any way you like in each of these projects, and I hope you'll consider including some of your own original block designs as well.

Use some of the beautiful blocks in the Anna Putney Farrington quilt as the basis for designing blocks that reflect your quiltmaking talents. Explore the rich vein of designs in other nineteenth-century appliqué quilts, as well, and enjoy the freedom that comes from creating your own unique artful album quilts.

Happy stitching!

Jane Townswick

UPDATING VINTAGE APPLIQUÉ DESIGNS

Reading Carla Hassel's book *Super Quilter II* inspired me to think about how I could enlarge vintage appliqué shapes to create new block designs. The first design I created in this way is the Peach Tree block below.

There are obvious similarities between Anna Putney Farrington's peach-tree design and mine; each block features four birds and six peaches. In my block, however, I used a velvet-looking, hand-painted Skydyes fabric by Mickey Lawler for five of the fruits and a yellow-green for the sixth. I also rounded the leaves and made them slightly larger. The result is an updated design that builds on the charm and beauty of the original.

Compare the blocks in the top row, opposite. While these two Mirror Images designs are similar, they are not identical. The positions and shapes of the flowers and leaves are alike; however, I added more vertical bars inside the vase and made them narrower. I also chose blue hand-painted fabrics to make the flowers at the sides of the block more prominent.

Another block from Anna's quilt inspired me to create my Blooming Cactus block (middle row, opposite). Compare the blocks and notice the differences. The vintage block features a red-and-green color scheme, which I departed from to stitch blossoms ranging from fiery peach to yellow, with a single, just-for-fun blue bud. I also omitted one of the blossom shapes in the original block and included only a few of the buds. I used the same vase shape as in the vintage block, but I rounded out the three large leaves.

Occasionally I need to change the set of a vintage block to suit a quilt I'm making. In the bottom row on the facing page, the vintage design is set on-point. I changed it to a straight-set block, used the same number of tulip shapes, and positioned the stems wider apart to fill the square space better.

Vintage Peach-Tree block

My Peach-Tree block

Vintage Mirror Images block

My Mirror Images block

Vintage Cactus block

My Blooming Cactus block

Vintage Tulips block

My Spring Tulips block

Sometimes a vintage album block can function as a starting point for a creative design of your own. For example, what I loved about the vintage block shown below left was the three chunky roses and the large, curved vase. I incorporated variations of those shapes in my block, omitting the vase handles and changing the slant of the lower openings in each flower to point upward like a smile. I then surrounded the roses with leaves and floral shapes that were related, but not identical, to the ones in the original design.

These are just a few ways you can create your own unique album blocks based on vintage appliqué designs. Spend some time looking closely at the blocks in the Anna Putney Farrington quilt on page 6 and see if you can see things that inspired some of the blocks in my quilt "Way Beyond Baltimore!" Use the steps that follow to design and stitch your own artful album blocks and borders based on photos of any vintage quilts that inspire you. The most important thing is to work *only* with antique quilts that are in the public domain—never with any designs created and copyrighted by a quilt designer or artist.

Vintage Baltimore block

My Beyond Baltimore block

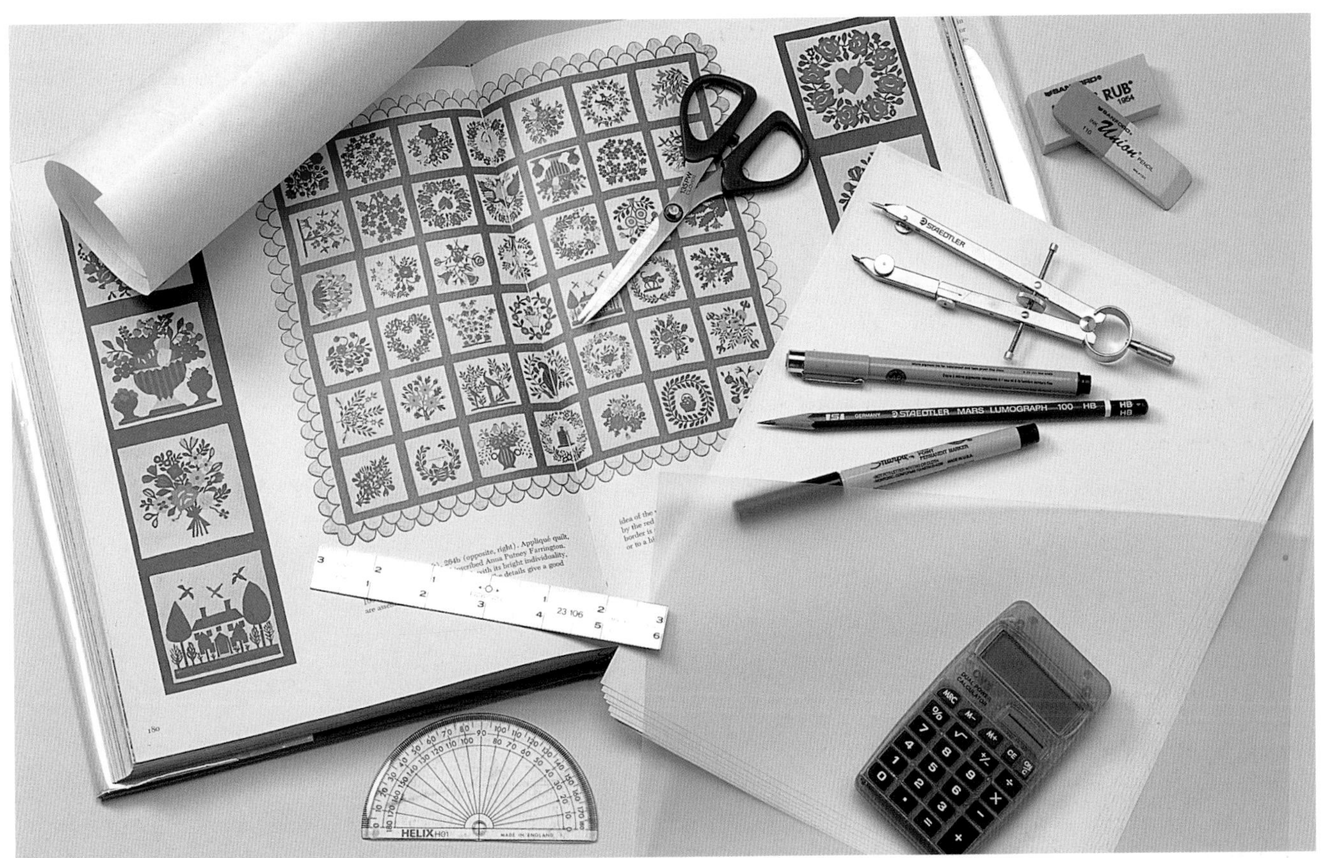

Getting Started

IN THIS SECTION you'll learn how to take a few easy measurements in any photo of an antique block and use them to enlarge the appliqué shapes to fit any size block you want to make. I first encountered information about this technique in the book *Super Quilter II*, by Carla J. Hassel. This method will free you from ever needing printed patterns again. All you need for starters are some photos of vintage appliqué blocks you like, the simple math formula that follows, and a willingness to do some creative paper cutting. The tools and supplies below will put you on the road to designing your own artful album quilts.

Tools and Supplies

- Photos of vintage appliqué quilts
- Calculator
- 6" ruler with 1/32" markings
- Plain white paper
- Freezer paper
- #2 pencil
- Eraser
- Sharpie permanent marking pen
- Compass
- Protractor
- Template plastic
- Scissors for paper and template plastic

Doing the Math

I USED THE following process to update blocks in the Anna Putney Farrington quilt. You can create your own block designs based on blocks from the same quilt, or use photos of any other vintage appliqué blocks that appeal to you. When you decide on an antique block to update, follow these steps to enlarge and adapt the shapes to fit whatever size quilt block you choose.

1. *Measure the vintage-block photo.* You can work with almost any size photo, even one as small as ½" square. If the photo measurement is a whole number, use that number throughout the following steps. If the photo measurement contains a fraction of an inch, convert the fraction to a decimal. To do this, simply divide the top number of the fraction by the bottom number. For example, to convert a block that measures ⅞" square to a decimal, divide the top number 7 by the bottom number 8 to get the decimal .875".

$7 \div 8 = .875''$

2. *Decide on your finished block size.* If your finished block measurement is a whole number, use that number in the following steps. If your finished block measurement contains a fraction of an inch, convert the fraction to a decimal as in step 1. For example, the decimal equivalent of a 9½" block is 9.5".

3. *Find the factor.* The factor is an important number. It expresses the relationship between the two block sizes. To find the factor, divide your finished block size by the size of your vintage-block photo. For example, to make a 14" finished block from a vintage block shown in a ⅞" square photo:

$$\frac{14''\ \text{(your finished block size)}}{.875''\ \text{(size of vintage-block photo)}} = 16\ \text{(the factor)}$$

The factor tells you that any appliqué shape shown in the ⅞" photo will need to be 16 times larger to be proportional in your 14" finished block.

NOTE: *This particular example uses a factor that is a whole number; however, the factor can also be a decimal, depending on your block measurements.*

4. *Measure the appliqué shapes in the vintage-block photo.* To take accurate measurements, especially in small block photos, use a 6" ruler that has 1⁄32" markings. Then convert your measurements to decimals.

   For shapes that are based on equal divisions of a circle, such as flowers, all you need to measure is the diameter of the circular area that the flower occupies in the photo. For symmetrical shapes such as leaves or vases, measure both the height and width of the shape. For asymmetrical shapes such as trees or birds, measure the height and width that the shape covers (and later divide the shape into sections, referring to "Asymmetrical Shapes" on page 16). For example, here are the height and width of a tulip in a vintage-block photo, along with the decimal conversions of each measurement.

Vintage tulip width	3⁄16" =	.1875"
Vintage tulip height	¼" =	.25"

If you're working with a very small block photo, try looking through an artist's loupe while you measure individual shapes. The magnification will make it easy to take accurate measurements.

5. Multiply the decimal measurements of the appliqué shape times the factor to determine the new size for each shape. For the tulip shape in step 4, multiply the decimal by the factor 16.

Tulip width	.1875" x 16 = 3"
Tulip height	.25" x 16 = 4"

This means that the width and height of the tulip in your 14" block should cover an area that measures 3" x 4".

Creating Your Own Appliqué Templates

After you have determined the proportional size each appliqué shape will need to be for your finished block size, you're ready to start creating your appliqué templates. This is where the fun begins! Cutting out a selection of appliqué shapes from freezer paper and combining them in creative ways is the basis for designing your original album blocks.

Shapes Based on Squares

1. For appliqué shapes that have the same height and width measurement, cut a square of freezer paper that same size.

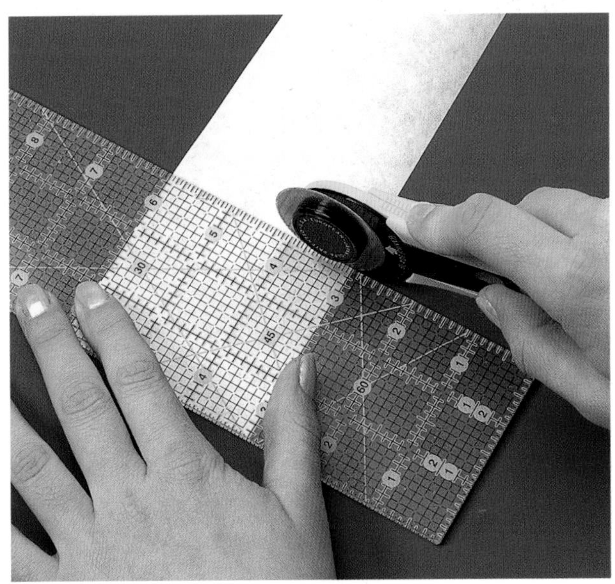

For simple shapes, like leaves and vases, try skipping the sketching phase entirely and simply cut out the shape freehand from a folded piece of freezer paper. Stack several layers of freezer paper on top of each other and rotary cut an appropriately sized square or rectangle through all layers. You'll instantly have several freezer paper rectangles in the appropriate size for whatever shape you want to create.

2. Fold the square in half with the shiny sides of the freezer paper together. Using a pencil, roughly sketch in the curves of the tulip on half of the freezer paper, starting and ending at the fold. Use the vintage-block photo as a guide or shape your tulip differently if you like. As long as it fills the 3" x 4" space, any tulip you create will look proportionally correct for a 14" finished block.

3. With the freezer paper still folded, freehand-cut the tulip, using your sketched lines as a guide. Open the cut shape and see how you like it. Cut out several freezer-paper tulips and see which ones appeal to you the most.

Save all of the templates you cut; they're bound to come in handy for future appliqué designs.

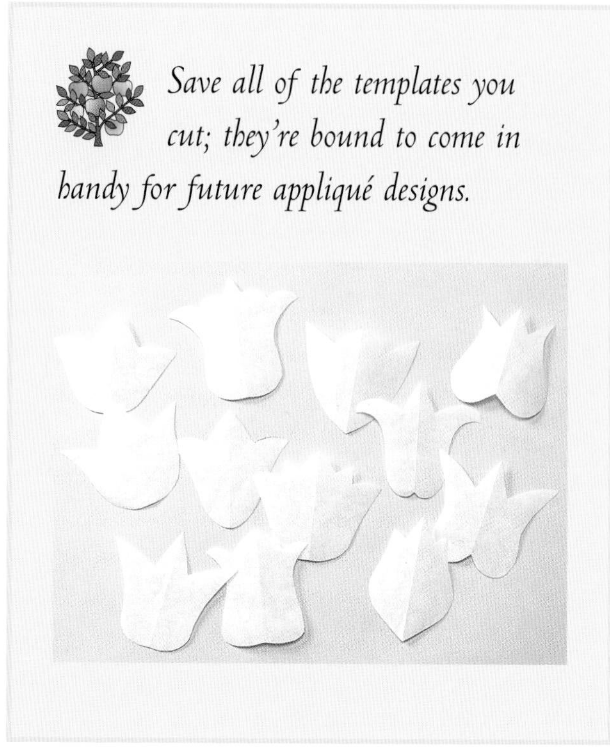

Shapes Based on Rectangles

Many leaf shapes are symmetrical and easy to cut from a freezer-paper rectangle. To create the large scalloped leaf shape in the Blooming Cactus block shown on page 86, I measured the height and width of the leaf shape in the vintage block photo and calculated the size the leaf should be for my 14" finished block. Then I drew a rectangle that size on freezer paper. Sketching in the scalloped curves was easy to do by eye on the folded rectangle, and cutting both layers of freezer paper at once resulted in this symmetrical leaf shape.

Most vases are symmetrical and easy to cut from a freezer-paper rectangle. Measure the vase in the vintage photo and determine the size rectangle that will accommodate the shape. Fold the freezer paper in half, sketch in the lines of the vase and base by eye, and cut the vase template out freehand.

Most of the leaves in each block have slightly different shapes. This comes from using a wooden toothpick to shape the leaves as you stitch. For a block pattern, choose one or two leaf shapes that appeal to you and use those to make the templates for all of the leaves in that design.

Shapes Based on Circles

1. Many flowers, such as the rose shown in the Beyond Baltimore block on page 90, are based on equal divisions of a circle. To create a template for any circular flower shape, measure the flower in the vintage block photo and determine how large a circle you will need to draw for the flower in your finished block size. Use a protractor to divide the circle into as many sections as you need. Sketch the curved petals in each section by eye or by using a circle stencil.

For very large flower shapes, use an artist's flexible curve to mark curved petals in each section of the freezer-paper template.

2. Cut out an array of flower shapes. When you create a shape that is particularly pleasing, make a template for that shape from template plastic, so you can feature it in more than one of your designs.

Asymmetrical Shapes

Some shapes do not fit neatly into the dimensions of a square, rectangle, or circle. You can draft shapes like these by following the same method used for any other type of shape. To create the template for the large bird in the Peacocks in a Tree block (page 106), I measured the height and width of the bird in the photo. Then I calculated the size freezer paper rectangle I needed to make this shape for a 14" finished block. I divided the rectangle in half in both directions so I could sketch the curves of the bird's body by eye. When I was happy with my sketched lines, I put another piece of freezer paper over my drawing and smoothed out the lines to create the final bird shape.

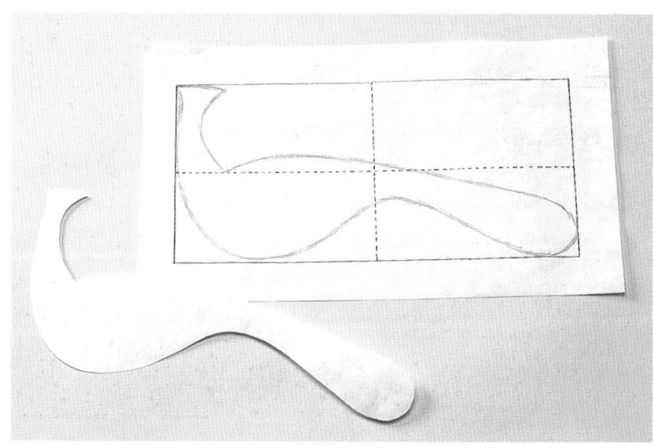

Stems and Vines

Measure the width of a stem or vine in your vintage block photo and calculate how wide it should be for your finished block. I decided to make the stems in all of my blocks ¼" wide. When you design your album blocks, choose your favorite stem width, as I did, or use different widths from block to block as desired.

Arranging Your Block Designs

1. Cut a square of fabric in your finished block size (without seam allowances) and place it on a flat surface. I like to use a dark fabric so that freezer-paper templates show up well.
2. Position large or central shapes, using the vintage block photo as a guide. You can determine the exact positions of shapes by measuring how far in the shape lies from the edges of the block in the photo and then calculating the correct position for your finished block. For this vase, I measured the vintage block photo and calculated that it should be positioned 1½" up from the bottom edge of my block.

3. If a vintage block features stems or vines, cut strips of freezer paper in the appropriate widths and lengths and position them on the fabric square by eye, or determine their exact positions as for any other appliqué shape.

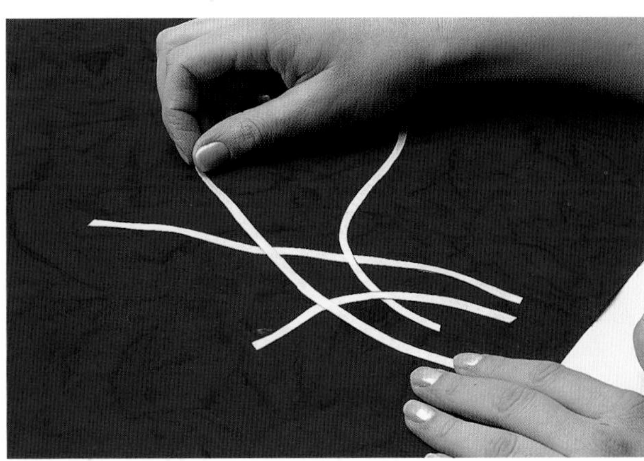

4. Position your remaining appliqué shapes on the background square by eye, following the layout of the vintage block, or change the positions as you desire. Be creative! It's fun to reproduce a vintage block design, but it is also enjoyable to do your own interpretation. Omit any shapes you don't care for in the original, or introduce new shapes that are not part of the vintage block. The only rule is to let your imagination take over and have fun. When you are happy with the positions of your freezer paper shapes, press them in place on the fabric square using a dry iron on the cotton setting.

5. Place your final design on top of a light box and lay a piece of freezer paper or butcher paper on top. Trace the design onto the freezer paper using a permanent marking pen. This creates a master block pattern that you can keep for future use. Build a library of your master block patterns so you can use them in various combinations and as a source of appliqué shapes for many different projects.

Combine your own block designs with some of the blocks in this book, or make an original album quilt using only your original designs.

A completed Crimson Blossoms block, made from the master pattern shown at left. For readymade template patterns, see pages 62–64.

ARTFUL APPLIQUÉ TECHNIQUES

ANY APPLIQUÉ PROJECT is more enjoyable when you use supplies and techniques that give you results you like. Here are some of the fabrics, tools, supplies, and techniques I count on to give me stitching success every time. The techniques that follow include an easy way to gain perfect control over your needle and thread, how to start and end a line of stitching invisibly, how to do tiny appliqué stitches, my method for perfect-bias stems and vines using a hera marker, how to do cutwork and reverse appliqué, and my new technique for appliquéing steep points (even points that feature two fabrics).

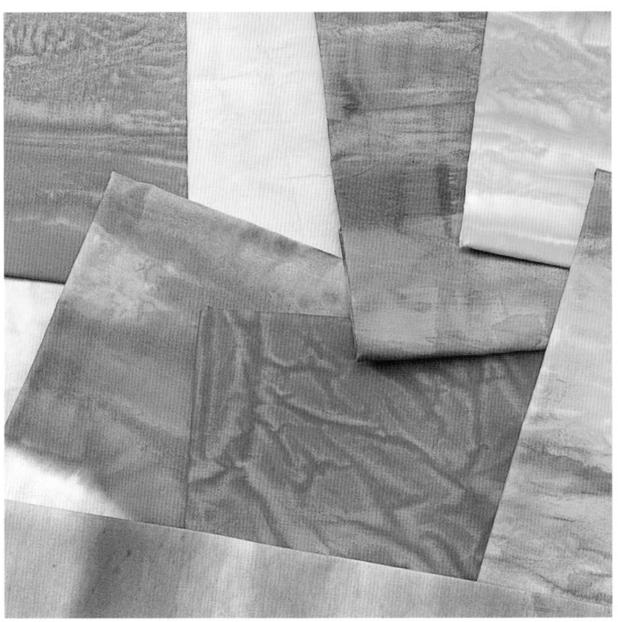

Mickey Lawler's Skydyes

Fabrics

TODAY'S ARRAY OF cotton fabrics for hand appliqué is widening each season to include even more beautiful choices. My favorites continue to be Mickey Lawler's Skydyes, which are one-of-a-kind, hand-painted masterpieces that put an entire palette of artistic colors at your fingertips. See "Resources" on page 125.

I also love the incredible range of colors in Fossil Fern prints by Benartex, Inc. Gail Kessler used these prints exclusively in her quilt "Pennsylvania Flower Garden" (page 48). Seta Wehbe also used them in the sashing strips of her quilt "Rhapsody in Red and Black" (page 52). See "Resources" on page 125.

Benartex fossil fern prints

Cotton batiks will always be an important part of my quilts because of their luscious colors and closely woven fibers. And silks add a subtle sheen that I find appealing, so I tend to buy them in every color I can find. If you use silk douppioni for your album blocks, be sure to interface the wrong side with lightweight, tricot fusible interfacing for stability.

Vibrant silks and batiks

Tools and Supplies

KEEP A WELL-stocked supply of the tools and equipment you like best for hand appliqué. Here is my list of appliqué essentials. Because appliqué is a continually developing art form, I'll no doubt be adding to this list as new products become available. For more information on these products, see "Resources" on page 125.

Template Materials

I like to use freezer paper for making templates for large appliqué shapes, as well as for shapes that I plan to stitch once, or just a few times. For repeated shapes, like leaves or flowers, I like to make templates out of medium-weight template plastic for greater durability.

Marking Pens and Pencils

For marking appliqué shapes on template plastic or freezer paper, nothing beats an ultra-fine Sharpie marker, which won't smear or come off on your fingers. I like using a .01mm Pigma marking pen for marking light- to medium-colored fabrics and a white Pentel Milky Gel Roller pen for marking dark fabrics. White and silver Quilter's Choice pencils are also great for marking appliqué shapes or quilting designs.

Threads

I am a big fan of YLI #100 silk thread, which is a filament so fine that it seems to glide through fabric almost without leaving a hole. It is available in a wide selection of colors, some of which are neutral enough to work with almost any color fabric you might want to use. Try using #235, #239, and #242 and see how you like them with the fabrics in your stash. Consider building a collection a few spools at a time, until you own all of the available shades, and you'll probably never want to stitch with any other thread.

Scissors

For cutting paper or plastic templates, use a pair of utility or craft scissors with blunt tips.

To cut appliqué shapes and clip seam allowances with precision, try using 3½" Gingher embroidery scissors with a serrated blade, which grips fabric better than non-serrated blades.

Beeswax and Thread Conditioner

To keep any type of thread from tangling, run an individual strand through a small cake of natural beeswax or a silicone-based thread conditioner like Thread Heaven. Either one will coat the thread, making it fray and twist less.

Needles

You'll enjoy greater stitching success when you use a needle that you really like. My favorites are the size #11 straw needle from Jeanna Kimball's Foxglove Cottage, and the size #12 Sharp from Mulberry Silk & Things. Both of these needles will help you easily create tiny, almost invisible stitches.

Needle Threaders

I like to try every new brand of needle threader I can find, from generic ones to the super-fine Clover double needle threaders that make it possible to thread a size 12 Sharp easily in any light.

Thimbles

Comfort is the keyword when it comes to wearing a thimble for any kind of hand stitching. I like wearing a metal thimble that has a slightly raised lip around the top, which gives me greater control over the eye of a needle. Whatever type of thimble you choose, make sure that it fits comfortably, without binding or constricting your finger, and that the tip of your finger does not press against the inside of the thimble as you stitch.

Straight Pins

Any straight pin you like using will work to secure appliqué pieces in position on a background square. I like long, thin, silk pins because they do not leave large holes in fabric. You can also find several brands of ¾"-long pins that are made especially for hand appliqué. Some brands of these shorter pins have white heads, which makes them easy to spot on furniture, floors, or carpeting, while others have smaller metal heads. If you're like me, you might enjoy trying out several different types to see which ones you like best.

Wooden Toothpicks

If there were suddenly no more wooden toothpicks in the world, I probably would not be able to do any more hand appliqué. My current favorites are small, 4"-long bamboo skewers, which are extremely strong and have very narrow, pointed tips. They grip the edge of an appliqué shape like no needle ever could, which is the secret to stitching smooth curves and sharp points. Bamboo skewers are available in grocery and kitchen-supply stores.

Hera Marker

My method for cutting and preparing perfect-bias stems and vines in any length or width is only possible with the use of a hera marker. This small, white, plastic tool has a curved, sharp edge at one end that allows you to score perfectly straight lines in fabric. In addition to making it a snap to create perfect-bias stems and vines, a hera marker is also great for marking straight quilting lines.

Sandpaper Board

I like doing hand appliqué with a sandpaper board in my lap, because the board's nonslip surface makes it easy to position appliqué shapes accurately on the background fabric.

Rotary-Cutting Equipment

You can use any size rotary-cutting mat you like that allows you to cut blocks and borders easily. I keep a very large Omnigrid mat on my kitchen table, which enables me to cut at a comfortable height and protects the tabletop. A rotary cutter with a sharp blade is a must for cutting the blocks and borders in this book. An acrylic ruler that measures 16½" square is useful for cutting background squares that are slightly larger than necessary. That way you can trim them to 14½" square later after you finish stitching. A 6" x 24" acrylic ruler is helpful for cutting long border strips.

Light Box

You may wish to use a light box for tracing the appliqué designs in this book onto your background fabric, especially if you choose a dark color. If you do not have access to a light box, you can use a sunny window with equal success.

Anchoring a Needle and Thread

When you have perfect control over your needle and thread, you'll enjoy a feeling of freedom when you do hand appliqué. Here is a technique that beaders and silk-ribbon embroiderers love for anchoring a thread onto the eye of a needle.

1. Thread a needle with an approximately 18" strand of thread. Holding the needle in your right hand, pick up the short end of the thread with your left thumb and forefinger. Lay the thread over the fingernail of your left index finger, bringing it around your finger, and grasp the longer part of the thread with the short end.

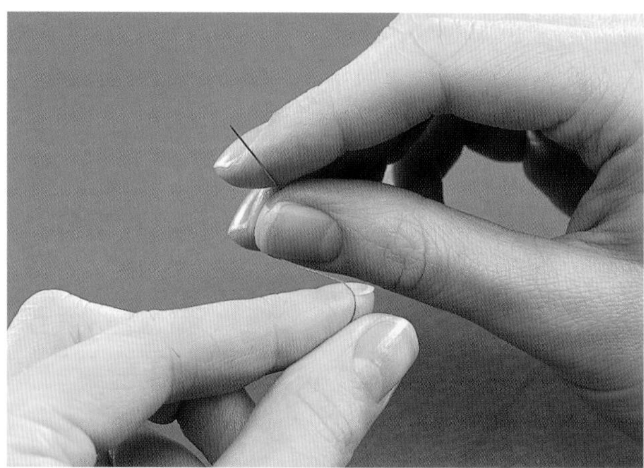

2. With the needle in your right hand, hold the thread in your left hand tightly so that it stays taut across your index fingernail. Point the tip of the needle at the thread. Slide the needle across the surface of your fingernail so that the tip of the needle *just* pierces the thread; then stop pushing the needle immediately.

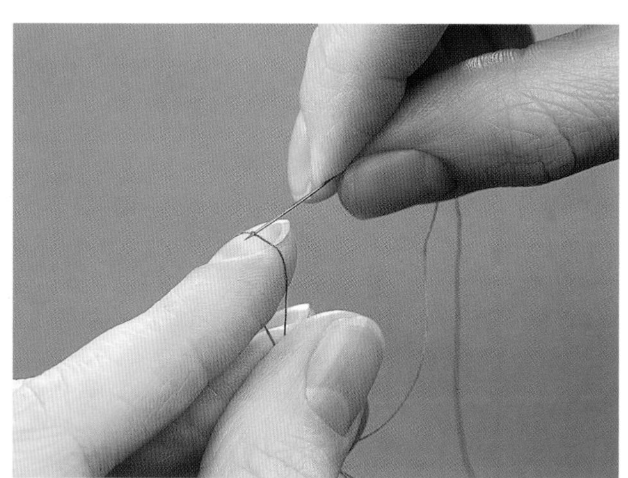

3. Pick up the needle tip with your left hand, and gently pull the thread along the shank of the needle with your right hand. This will lock the thread securely onto the eye of the needle. This is not a knot. When you anchor a needle and thread in this way, you'll be in complete control of the needle and thread as you stitch. The needle will stay in the same place on the thread until you release it. You won't ever lose another needle, and you'll be able to work with more of the actual thread length because the needle is anchored close to the short end of the thread.

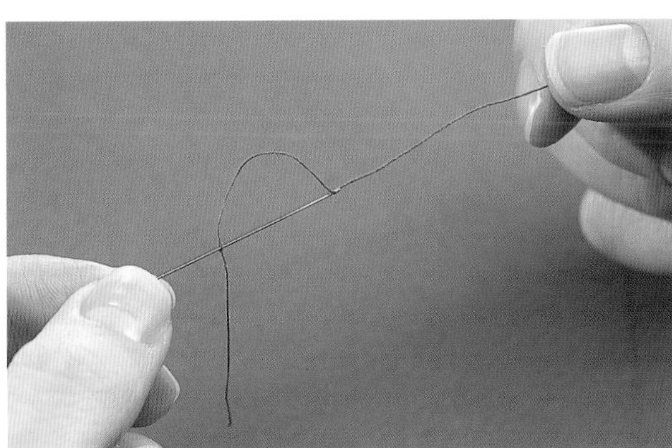

4. Make a small quilter's knot at the long end of the thread. Hold the needle and the long end of the thread together in your right hand. With your left hand, wind the thread gently around the needle two or three times. Slide the wound portion of thread down the shank of the needle so that it lodges between your right thumb and forefinger.

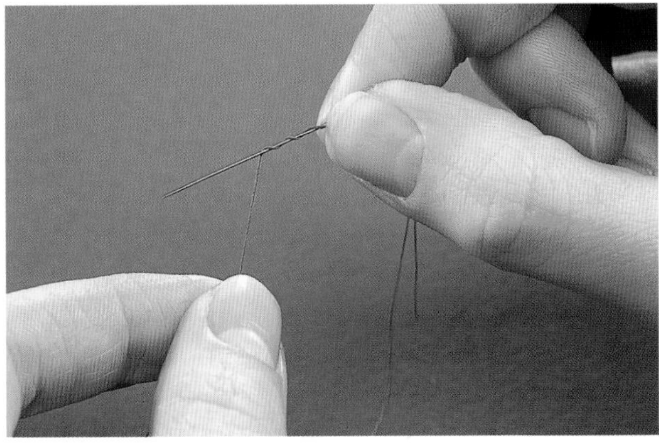

5. With your left hand, gently pull the needle up while still holding the wound threads between your right thumb and forefinger. Continue pulling the needle until the wound portion of thread forms a small knot at the end of the thread.

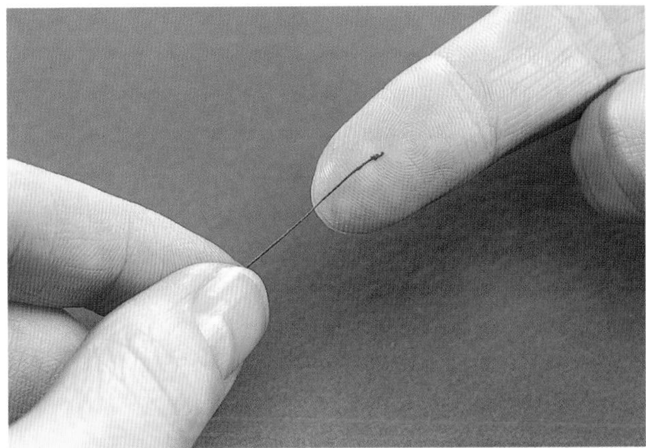

Tiny Appliqué Stitches

1. After anchoring a strand of thread on a needle and knotting the thread, bring the needle up just inside the marked turning line of an appliqué shape, away from a point or a deep inner curve.

2. Use the tip of a wooden toothpick to turn under the fabric so that the turning line is just out of sight. The rough surface of the wood will grab the seam allowance, giving you better control over the fabric. When you're happy with the way the fold looks, lightly crease it with your left thumbnail, creating a crisp, easy-to-stitch edge about ¼" long.

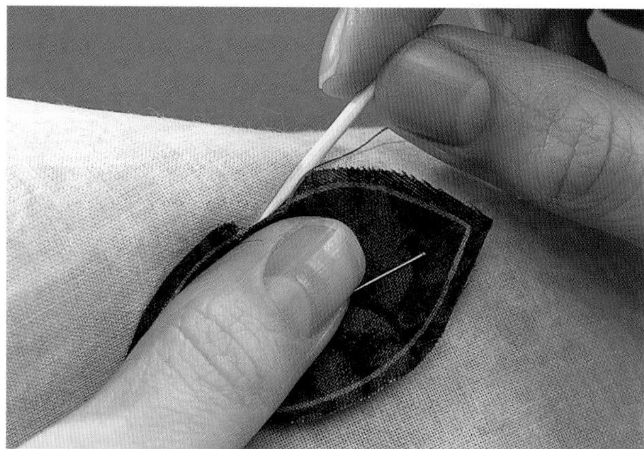

3. To start the first stitch, pull the thread out at a right angle to the fold. Insert the tip of the needle into the background fabric to the right of where the thread exits the appliqué shape.

4. Bring the needle up through the background fabric a short distance to the left, just catching the edge of the appliqué shape. Catch only one or two threads of the fold. This step determines your stitch length, which, in my experience, is different for almost everyone. I enjoy making tiny stitches (approximately 20 to 24 or more per inch) because they allow me to stitch smoother curves and sharp points. Determine the stitch length you prefer and stick with whatever length feels comfortable and gives you results you like.

5. Bring the needle all the way through the fabric and pull the thread out again at a right angle to determine where to insert the needle for your next stitch. Continue stitching in the same manner, taking care to keep the intervals between your stitches even.

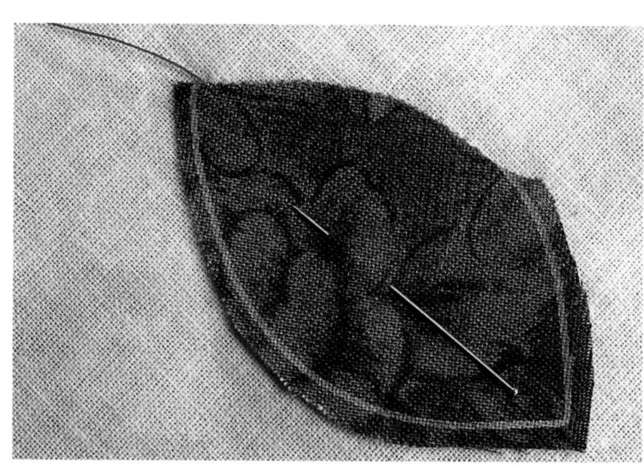

6. To end a thread, insert the needle into the background fabric as though you were going to take another stitch, but bring it all the way through to the wrong side. Wind the thread around your needle two or three times, and insert the tip of the needle between the background fabric and appliqué shape underneath. Tug gently on the thread so that the wound portion lodges around the needle at the surface of the background fabric.

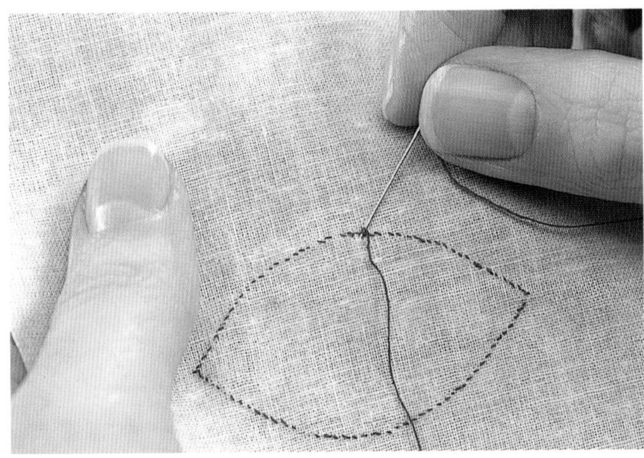

7. Pull the needle and thread all the way out of the background fabric. Tug gently on the thread so the knot pops out of sight and lodges between the background fabric and the appliqué shape. Clip the thread close to the surface of the fabric.

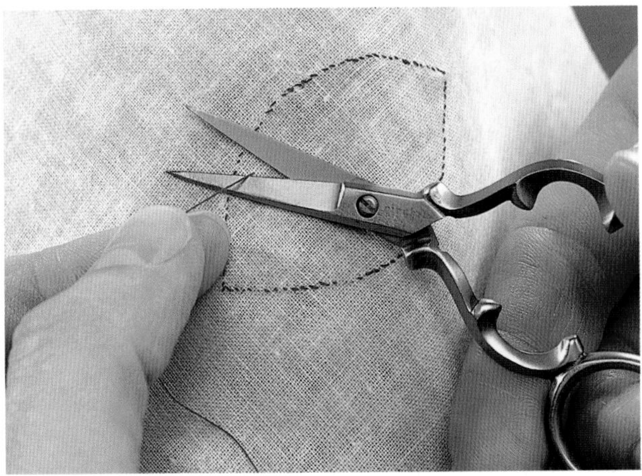

Bias Stems

For any appliqué design that features bias stems or vines, try my method for making perfect-bias strips with a hera marker and a rotary cutter. It is a super-quick way to prepare accurate bias strips from ⅛" up to any width you desire and as long or as short as you wish.

1. Start with a piece of fabric large enough to accommodate the bias strips in the length and width you need. Place the fabric wrong side up on top of a rotary cutting mat. Align the 45°-angle line on an acrylic ruler with the fabric's selvage edge and rotary cut a true bias edge.

In addition to making great stems and vines, this technique is also wonderful for making bias strips for Celtic or stained glass appliqué.

2. Move the ruler ⅛" to the right of the cut bias edge. Using a hera marker, score a line right next to the ruler's edge, pressing down *very hard* as you move the hera marker slowly back and forth. This will score a perfectly straight line that will be the first fold of the bias strip.

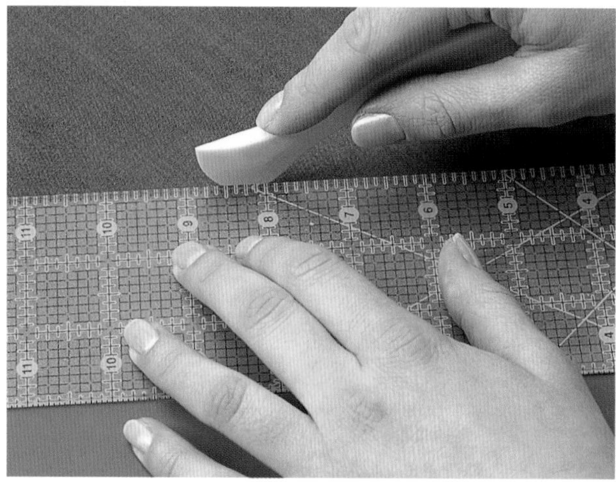

3. Move the ruler to the right of the first scored line, the same distance as the *finished width* of your stem or vine. For the blocks in this book the stems are ¼" wide; if you want yours to be the same, move the ruler ¼" to the right of the first scored line. Use the hera marker to score a second straight line in the same manner as the first. This scored line will be the second fold of the bias stem.

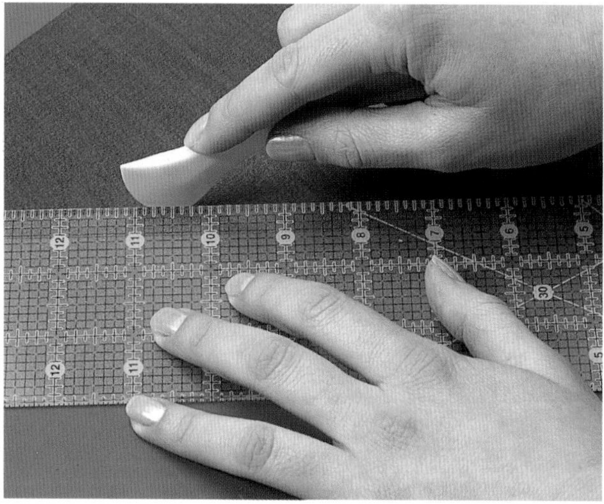

4. Move the ruler ⅛" to the right of the second scored line and rotary cut the fabric. This completes a ¼" bias strip with two ⅛" seam allowances.

The neat thing about this technique is that when you stitch this type of stem or vine in place, the seam allowances will automatically turn under in the right direction because you scored the turning lines with the wrong side of the fabric facing up.

Cutwork and Reverse Appliqué

Use cutwork appliqué for any design where you want to position a shape accurately on the background fabric. Choose reverse appliqué wherever you want a lower layer of fabric to show through an opening in an upper layer of fabric. These techniques are likely to become two of your favorite methods for stitching tricky shapes accurately.

The following blocks feature various shapes that are stitched with cutwork appliqué: Scalloped Tulip Wreath (page 56), Circle of Teardrops (page 65), Carnations and Tulips (page 98), and Lyre Wreath (page 110). Designs featuring reverse appliqué include: Crimson Blossoms (page 61), Mirror Images (page 71), Vintage Vase (page 75), Spring Tulips (page 82), Beyond Baltimore (page 90), Carnations and Tulips (page 98), and Lyre Wreath (page 110).

1. To stitch this Circle of Teardrops wreath using cutwork appliqué, trace the entire wreath shape onto a piece of freezer paper, including the small openings in the leaf shapes. Cut out the freezer-paper template on the drawn lines and press it onto a square of top fabric the same size as your background square. Mark around the template with a fabric-marking pen or pencil. Remove the freezer paper.

2. Pin the marked top fabric to your background square at each corner and at the center. Starting in the center, cut into the top layer of fabric *only*, leaving a 3/16" seam allowance 1" to 2" long inside the marked turning line.

3. Begin stitching the inner edge of the wreath to the background square. When you have stitched the distance of your cut seam allowance, cut another 1" to 2" portion of seam allowance and stitch that distance.

4. Work your way around the inner edge of the wreath, stitching only a short distance up the side of each leaf stem. Cut a 3/16" seam allowance around the leaf shape. Then begin stitching again on the opposite side of the stem. This will allow you to stitch the entire wreath in position while the leaf shapes remain free. That way you can add another layer of fabric underneath the leaf openings later.

5. After you have stitched the inner portion of the wreath in place, reverse appliqué the leaf openings. Pin a small piece of contrasting fabric underneath the leaf shape. Cut into one of the leaf openings through the top fabric only, and cut a 3/16" seam allowance inside the marked line. Clip the seam allowance, spacing the clips 1/8" apart, and stitch the leaf opening to the lower layer of fabric. Do the same for the second opening in the leaf shape.

6. Turn the leaf shape to the wrong side and trim the lower layer of fabric, leaving a 3/16" seam allowance. Repeat steps 5 and 6 to reverse appliqué each leaf shape in the Circle of Teardrops block. Stitch the outer edges of the leaves to the background fabric.

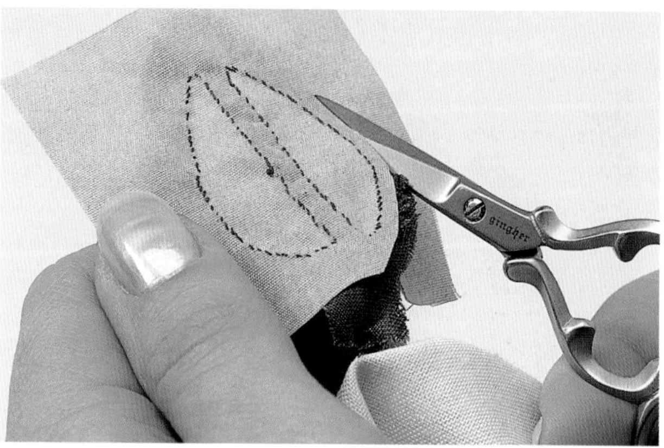

Getting to the Point!

Stitching very acute angles is tricky, no matter how long you've been a hand appliquér, because fabric doesn't always behave the way it should. This is especially true if the points are very steep, or if they feature two fabrics as in the arrowhead motifs in the "Way Beyond Baltimore!" border (page 114). Although I had already figured out some helpful tips and tricks for appliquéing most steep points, recently I worked out a new solution for very acute angles. After analyzing the problems involved in stitching points, I figured out that it is not the *first* side of an acute angle that causes trouble; you can easily stitch all the way up to the very tip of a point on the first side. It's that *second* side of a steep point that causes stitching chaos—fibers that fray, stray threads that pop out at the tip of the point, and seam allowances that cause too much bulk in a tiny space.

After giving it some thought, I developed a way to stitch the second side of a steep point in exactly the same way as the first side. All I did was reverse my stitching direction on the second side, and it worked the very first time I tried it! As I stitched various angles—even points that featured two fabrics—I realized that what I was doing was similar to a technique that appliqué artist and designer Nancy Pearson developed for stitching overlapping flower petals. For more information on Nancy's technique, refer to her book, *Floral Appliqué* (see "Bibliography" on page 126). Follow these steps to stitch the arrowhead motifs on page 114 or any other steep point, whether it features one or two fabrics.

1. Trace the arrowhead pattern from page 114, including the center line, onto a piece of template plastic, and cut it out on the marked lines.

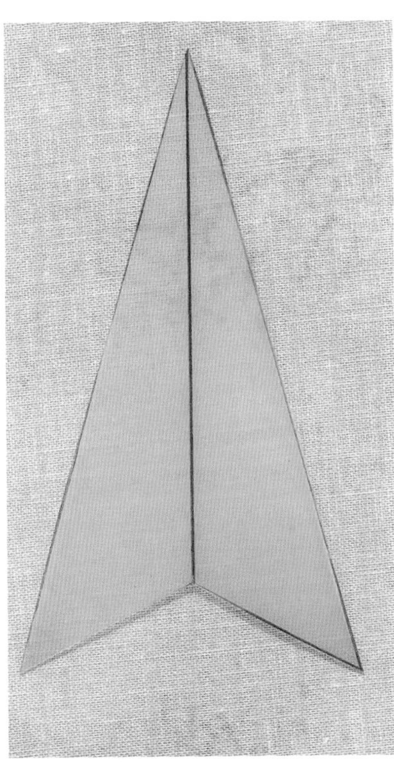

2. Cut two strips of fabric, each 2" x 5". With right sides together, *machine sew* the two strips of fabric together lengthwise with a 3/16" seam allowance. Decide which fabric you want on the left half of the finished arrowhead (when the single tip of the arrowhead is pointing upward). Press the seam allowance toward that fabric, so that you will be able to stitch the first side of the point without the seam allowance getting in your way.

For the arrowheads in the border of "Way Beyond Baltimore!" I used the same dark blue batik fabric in one half of each shape and chose a variety of purple prints for the other half. You can do the same, or choose different fabrics for both halves of the arrowheads.

3. Position the center line of the arrowhead template on top of the seam between the two strips of fabric and mark around the template.

4. Cut out the arrowhead with a *¼"-wide* seam allowance.

5. Clip the seam allowance on the *right* edge of the arrowhead, approximately 1" above the lower right point. When you do this, cut exactly *to*, but not *through*, the marked turning line. Using a water-soluble fabric gluestick, apply a thin layer of glue to the wrong side of the seam allowance and turn it under, forming a perfectly straight line all the way to the tip of the point.

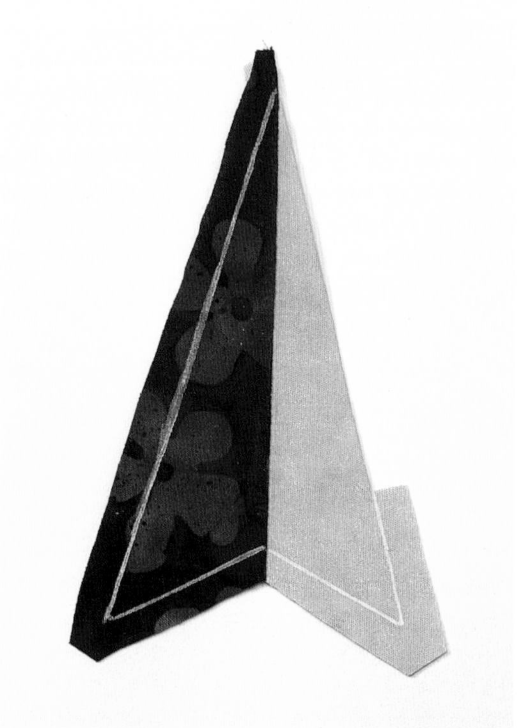

6. Repeat step 5 on the other edge of the arrowhead so that the glue-basted portion of the seam allowance begins approximately 1" from the upper point and ends at the lower left point.

7. Glue-baste the seam allowance from the center seam to the tip of the lower right point. To do this, you will need to release a few stitches of the center seam so that the seam allowance will turn under completely.

8. Pin the glue-basted arrowhead shape in position on the background fabric with straight pins. Appliqué the right (pink) edge of the arrowhead in place, starting at the beginning of the glue-basted area and ending at the very tip of the point.

   NOTE: *Do* not *end the thread when you reach the tip of the point; instead, move immediately to the next step.*

9. Insert the needle straight down into the background fabric at the very tip of the point, as if to take a stitch. Bring the thread through to the wrong side. Take one tiny lock stitch *directly on top* of your previous stitching, creating a loop of thread. Run the needle through this loop and pull on the thread until the stitch locks securely in place. Cut the thread, leaving a 3" to 4" tail hanging free.

   NOTE: *Do* not *clip the thread close to the surface of the fabric; you will need it to tie an anchoring knot later.*

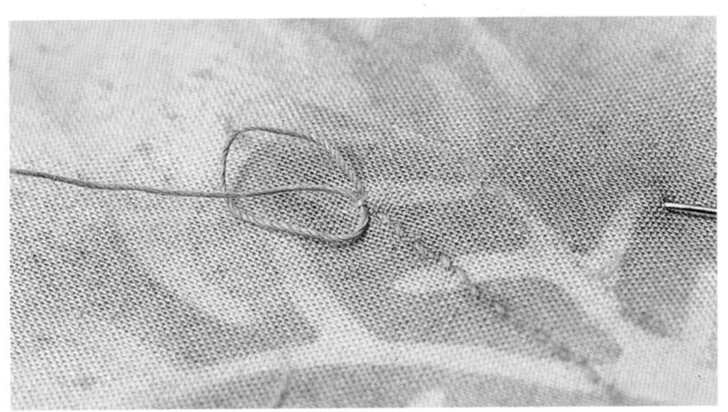

10. Turn your work to the right side and appliqué the other long edge of the arrowhead shape. When you reach the tip of the lower left point, insert the needle through the background fabric as before, bringing the thread through to the wrong side of your work. Take a tiny lock stitch, as before, to secure this line of stitching.

11. Stitch the third glue-basted edge of the arrowhead in the same way and do a lock stitch on the wrong side of your work as before. All three of the unbasted portions of seam allowance remain unstitched.

12. On the wrong side of your work, cut a ¼" seam allowance inside your stitched lines, taking care to cut through the background fabric *only*. This creates an opening inside the entire arrowhead.

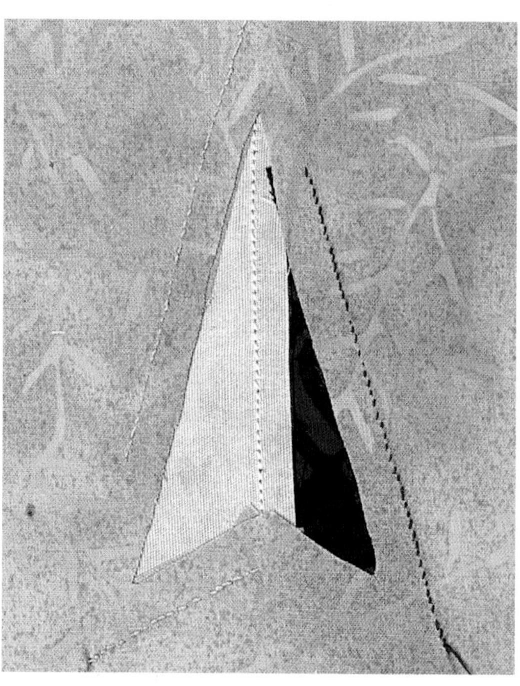

13. At the uppermost point of the arrowhead shape, and working on the wrong side of your work, cut the seam allowance straight up to the top stitch in your previously stitched line. Don't be afraid to do this—be brave and cut right up to your lock stitch!

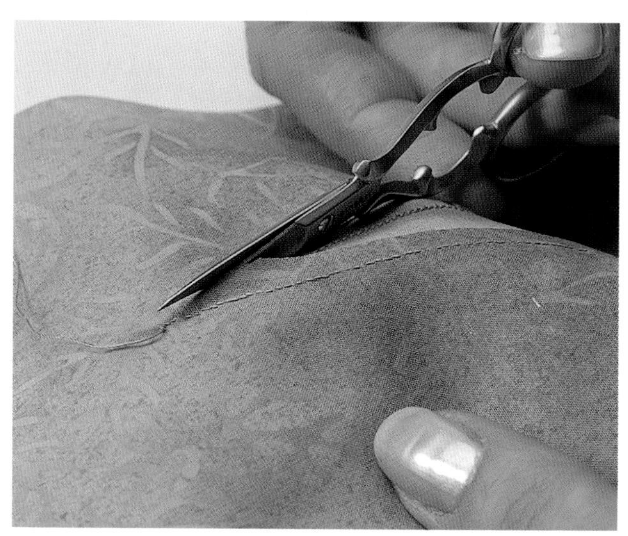

14. Clip the seam allowance, exactly to the point where your previous stitching ends. Fold the seam allowance over, as shown, creating a straight edge that goes from the tip of the point to exactly where your previous stitching on this side of the shape ended. Glue-baste this portion of the seam allowance, making sure to coat it well at the tip of the point.

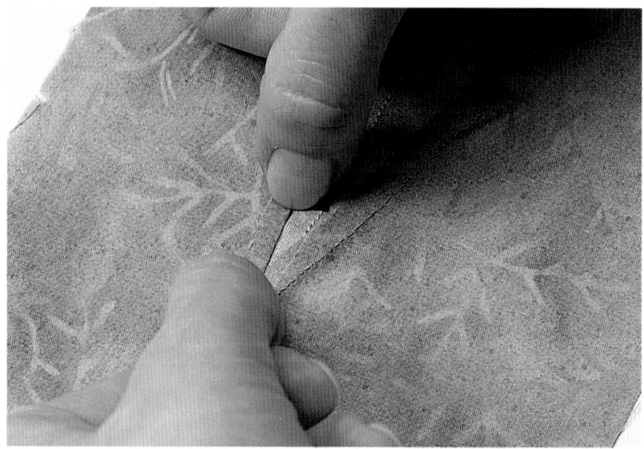

15. Use your fingers to push the unstitched portion of seam allowance gently through to the *wrong* side.

16. Following steps 12 through 15 will give you a perfectly straight, glue-basted fold on the left side of the arrowhead shape, on the right side of your work.

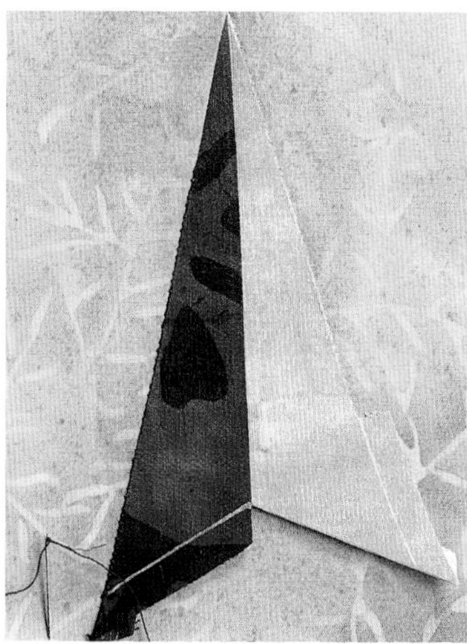

17. Insert your needle at the beginning of the glue-basted fold and stitch *toward* the tip of the point. This *reverses* the normal stitching direction for the second side of a point. The beauty of this method is that the bulk of this seam allowance will lie out of the way of the point after you finish stitching. When you reach the tip of the point, insert the needle through the background fabric and do a tiny lock stitch on the wrong side of your work, as before. The result of this step will be a perfect steep point that lies absolutely flat.

18. On the wrong side of your work at the very tip of the point, tie a knot using the thread on your needle and the other thread still hanging free. This will secure the stitches at the tip of the point. Tie another knot for extra security and clip the threads ¼" from the surface of the fabric.

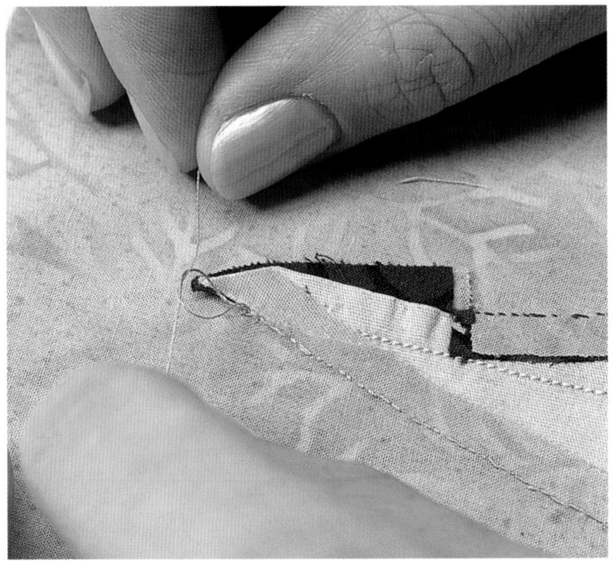

For stitching the arrowhead shape on page 114, use a neutral color of silk thread that blends with the fabrics you use. That way, you can cut down on the number of times you'll need to change thread colors.

19. To stitch the remaining portion of the lower left and right points of the arrowhead, repeat steps 13 through 18.

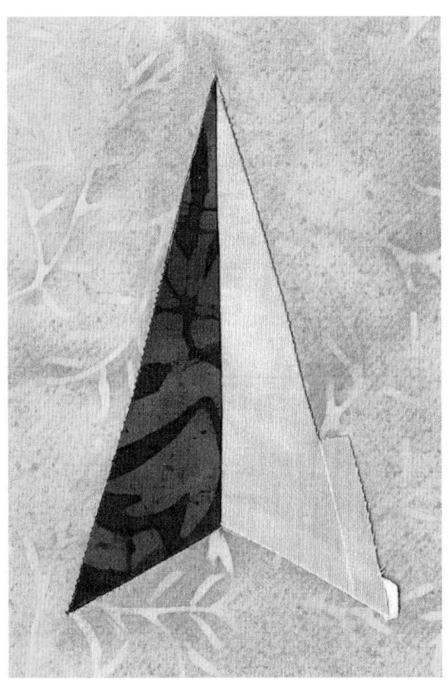

STITCHING THE BLOCKS

EACH OF THE three album quilts in this book features a different number and combination of blocks. "Way Beyond Baltimore!" on page 44 contains all sixteen designs. "Pennsylvania Flower Garden" on page 48 features twelve blocks, and "Rhapsody in Red and Black" on page 52 contains nine. Choose any blocks that appeal to you for making the nine- and twelve-block quilts, or expand your design options by following the techniques on pages 9–18 to create some original appliqué blocks of your own. Follow these guidelines for making the blocks in this book.

Templates for this Tree of Life block are included on pages 79–81. Read "Making Master Patterns" at right to get started.

Making Master Patterns

EACH BLOCK PATTERN in this book is shown in four sections, so you will need to make a master pattern to connect the sections. Using a black, permanent marking pen, trace each section from the book onto a 16" square piece of freezer paper, aligning the dashed placement lines accurately.

Another way to create a master block pattern is to use a photocopy machine that is 100% accurate to photocopy the sections that make up each pattern. Tape the photocopies together, matching placement lines, and use this as a master block pattern.

Preparing Background Fabrics

Cut your background squares 16" x 16". You will trim the blocks to 14½" x 14½" when your stitching is complete. To prepare light-colored background squares, fold the fabric in quarters to find the center. Place the background square on top of the master block pattern, matching the centers. Using a quilter's mechanical pencil or fabric-marking pencil, mark the positions of each appliqué shape in the design. For long, narrow shapes such as stems, I mark only one side of the stem or vine to use as the stitching line. For flowers, vases, trees, branches, birds, or other shapes, I mark as few lines as possible—just enough to indicate the correct positions or the directions that leaves should fall. Whatever kind of markings you make, stay well inside the outlines of the appliqué shapes so that the marks will not be visible after you finish stitching.

For dark background fabrics, tape the master block pattern to a light box and tape your background square over the master pattern, matching the center points, and mark where shapes should be positioned.

To prepare the background strips for the border of "Rhapsody in Red and Black," refer to the cutting list for that project. It explains how to cut the background strips ½" wider and ½" longer than necessary, so that you can trim them to the correct size after your appliqué is finished. The border strip dimensions in the cutting list for "Pennsylvania Flower Garden" include 2" extra length and 1" extra width for the same purpose. For "Way Beyond Baltimore!" follow the piecing instructions for each border unit and add the appliqué shapes to each pieced unit, referring to "Getting to the Point!" on pages 28–34.

Stitching Sequences

1. Start by positioning and appliquéing the stems or vines for any block or border, taking care to stitch accurately along the placement lines you marked on the background fabric. If a vine or stem is attached to a shape that will need to be reverse appliquéd, such as in the Circle of Teardrops block (page 65), leave those portions of the stem or vine unstitched until you can do the necessary reverse appliqué. Then stitch the reverse appliquéd portions to the background fabric.
2. Pin or baste the remaining appliqué shapes on the block or border background fabric. Make sure that the finished appliqués will cover all of the placement markings. Stitch the appliqués in place in any order you wish, taking care to stitch underlying shapes before you stitch the shapes that will overlap them.

Pressing and Trimming

1. To ensure that your finished blocks and borders will look crisp and flat, spray the wrong side of your work lightly with water and press the fabric with a hot, dry iron on the cotton setting. Mist the front side of your work with water and press again.
2. Place your finished blocks on top of a cutting mat. Use a rotary cutter and square acrylic ruler to trim them to 14½" square, making sure to center the design.
3. Press border strips in the same manner as blocks. Trim them to the width and length indicated in the project instructions, using the horizontal center lines on each border pattern as your guide.
4. Decide whether you want to do any hand quilting inside any of the larger appliqué shapes in your blocks and borders. If so, consider trimming away some of the background fabric underneath these shapes. This is optional, but it allows you to avoid hand quilting through multiple layers of fabric. To trim away the background fabric, separate the layers of fabric carefully and use a sharp pair of embroidery scissors to trim a ¼" seam allowance inside each appliqué shape on the wrong side of your work.

When the block size you want to make is more than 16" finished, it can be difficult to find an acrylic square ruler large enough to trim your blocks accurately with a rotary cutter. Consider contacting a local hardware store or glass company and having them cut a square of Plexiglas in the size square you need. Remember to include ½" for the seam allowances.

ASSEMBLING A QUILT TOP

FOLLOW THESE GUIDELINES to assemble your blocks and sashing strips into rows. Then join the rows to create the quilt center and add the borders, following the instructions in each project.

Machine Piecing

USE AN ACCURATE ¼" seam allowance for assembling your quilt top. If necessary, do a test to ensure that your seam allowances will be the correct width. Sew together two pieces of scrap fabric with the raw edges aligned with the right edge of your machine's presser foot. Measure the width of this seam allowance. If it is not exactly ¼", adjust the position of the needle and try again, or place a piece of masking tape exactly ¼" to the right of the needle on the bed of your sewing machine and use it as a seam guide.

Pressing

FOLLOW THE STANDARD rule of pressing seam allowances toward the darker of two fabrics whenever possible. If you are making a quilt that has sashing strips, press the block seam allowances toward the sashing strips when you assemble the quilt center so that you can quilt to the very edges of the blocks easily. After you have assembled the quilt center and added the borders, press the completed quilt top to make sure that the seam allowances lie consistently in the correct direction and to prepare it for layering and basting.

Pressing for a very large quilt top can be tricky on an ironing board that has diagonal edges at one end. For a larger surface that makes it easy to press even a bed-size quilt without wrinkles, puckers, or distortions, consider purchasing a Big Board. This 22" x 60" rectangular ironing board fits right over the top of a standard ironing board and lets you press a large quilt top evenly and quickly. *See "Resources" on page 125.*

QUILTING AND FINISHING

THE FOLLOWING GUIDELINES apply to hand quilting. If you wish to machine quilt your project, refer to *Machine Quilting Made Easy* by Maurine Noble for more information on machine quilting techniques.

Layering and Basting

1. Remove the selvage edges from the 2 lengths of backing fabric. Sew the lengths together with a ¼"-wide seam allowance. Press the backing with the seam allowance open to make it easier to hand quilt.
2. With the wrong side up, place the pressed backing on a flat surface such as a large table or floor. Center the batting of your choice on top, smoothing out any wrinkles. Place your pressed quilt top on top of the batting so that approximately 2" of batting and backing are visible on all sides.
3. Use white thread or safety pins to baste the 3 layers of the quilt sandwich together. White thread is best because the dye from colored threads may bleed into the fabric. You can thread-baste in a pattern of diagonal lines radiating outward from the center of the quilt, or in a straight-line grid, spacing your lines of basting stitches about 6" apart.

   If you like to pin-baste, choose small nickel-plated, rustproof, brass safety pins, which will not discolor the quilt over a long period of time. Place safety pins approximately 6" apart, working outward from the middle of the quilt in a grid-like pattern of straight lines.

My favorite size safety pin for basting a quilt is size #0 because it has a very thin shank that does not leave large holes in fabric.

Marking Methods

I LIKE TO mark as few quilting lines as possible on a quilt top, so there will be fewer marks to remove after the quilting is finished. Try these methods and see which ones you like best for your quilts.

PAPER AND PLASTIC TEMPLATES

An easy method for quilting isolated motifs is to trace the designs onto freezer paper, press them onto the quilt top, and quilt around the edges of the freezer paper. I have also used CAT paper with success. This product is an opaque plastic sheet that has adhesive on one side. You can trace a quilting design onto it with a permanent marking pen, cut the motif out, position it wherever you wish on your quilt top, and quilt around it. The advantage of CAT paper is that it does not need to be pressed onto the fabric with an iron, which makes it a great choice if you suddenly get a great quilting design idea when your quilt is already layered and basted. For more information on CAT paper, see "Resources" on page 125.

Low-Tack Masking Tape

For quilting grids of crosshatch lines in the background of an appliqué quilt, I like to use low-tack masking tape as guides. Place a long acrylic ruler diagonally, vertically, or horizontally on the quilt top for each gridline and place the tape next to the edge of the ruler. This makes it easy to quilt straight lines next to the tape. Ask for low-tack masking tape at paint stores.

Fabric-Marking Pencils

To mark an intricate quilting design, or one that has a number of disconnected lines, nothing beats Quilter's Choice silver and white pencils. They have strong cores of marking substance that are easy to sharpen and don't break easily. If you mark lightly on either dark or light fabrics, your quilting designs will be easy to see while you stitch, and virtually disappear after you have finished quilting. Whatever kind of fabric-marking pen or pencil you decide to use, make sure to test it for visibility and removability using actual fabrics from your quilt. This will allow you to mark quilting designs with confidence.

Echoing Appliqué Motifs

One of the things that can lend unity to a quilt is echoing some of the appliqué motifs in the quilting. In "Way Beyond Baltimore!" on page 44, I repeated the border arrowheads in the open areas where four sashing strips meet. Any of the flowers, birds, leaves, or other shapes in this quilt would also make interesting quilting motifs. Consider this concept for any appliqué album quilt you make, especially when you start creating your own block and border designs.

Filling Background Areas

Backgrounds in appliqué quilts can be closely quilted in diagonal or straight crosshatch patterns or feature isolated motifs that are combined with background quilting lines. The choices for quilting any project are limited only by your imagination. It is fun to look through books of antique quilts and analyze the quilting styles and designs that appeal to you and incorporate those ideas in your own projects.

Binding Methods

Double-fold binding was used on the "Way Beyond Baltimore!" and the "Pennsylvania Flower Garden" quilts. This is a traditional edge finish that is durable and always looks great. The "no-binding" binding used on the "Rhapsody in Red and Black" quilt is also a good choice any time you want a sleek, flat-looking edge treatment.

Double-Fold Binding

1. Trim the batting and backing fabric to ¼" from the edges of your quilt.
2. Cut the required number of binding strips for the quilt you are making. Sew the short ends of the strips right sides together, using diagonal seams. Trim these seams to ¼" and press them open.

3. With wrong sides together, fold the entire binding strip in half lengthwise and press.

4. Beginning away from a corner, leave approximately 6" of the binding hanging free and begin stitching the binding strip to the quilt using a ¼" seam allowance. Stop the seam exactly ¼" from the next corner.

5. Fold the binding fabric up and back down upon itself, creating a 45° fold at the corner. Insert the machine needle exactly at the point where your previous line of stitching ended and stitch the binding to the next side of the quilt, stopping ¼" from the next corner. Repeat for the remaining sides of the quilt, ending your line of stitching about 6" from the point where you began.

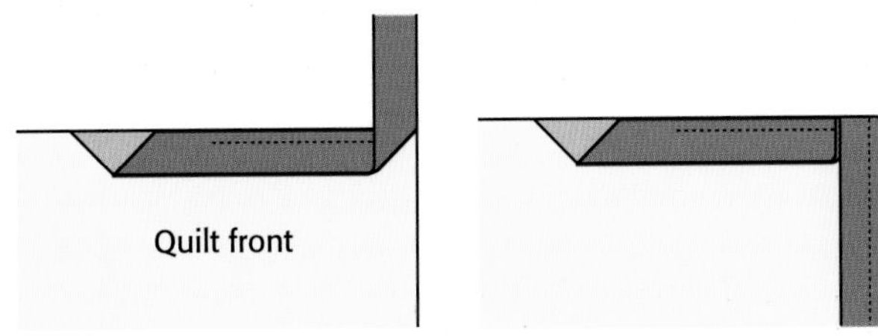

6. Fold the ends of the binding together so that they meet at a 45° angle. Finger-crease these folds, open the binding strips, and machine sew them together with a diagonal seam. Trim the seam allowance to ¼" and finger-crease it open.

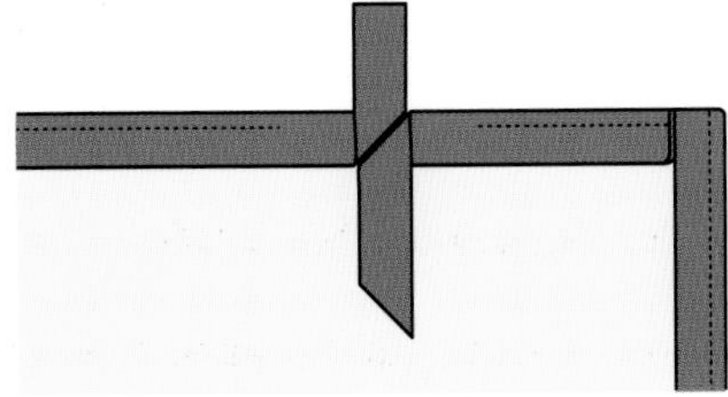

7. Fold the completed binding strip in half with wrong sides together and sew the remaining portion of the binding to the quilt.

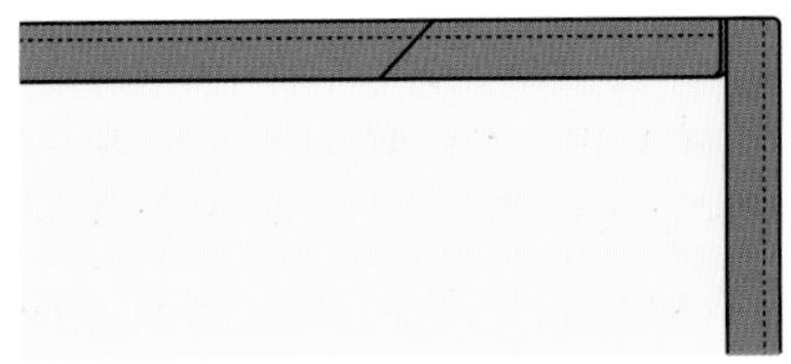

8. Fold the binding to the back side of the quilt and stitch it in place by hand, forming a 45° mitered fold at each corner. After the binding is completely stitched, stitch the mitered folds at each corner or leave them unstitched, whichever you prefer.

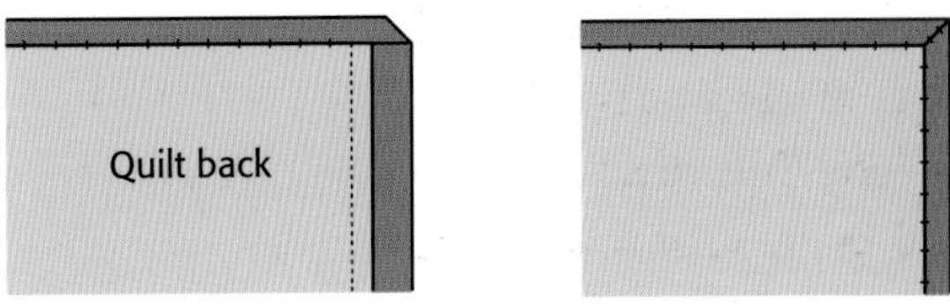

"No-Binding" Binding

1. Trim the batting and backing fabric to ¼" from the edges of your quilt top.

2. Measure your quilt top through the center. Cut two 2½"-wide binding strips this length and sew the short ends together, right sides together, using a ¼" seam allowance. Press this seam open. Fold the binding strip lengthwise, with wrong sides together, and press. Repeat to prepare the binding strips for the other three sides of the quilt in the same manner.

3. Using a ¼" seam allowance, sew a binding strip to one edge of the right side of the quilt. Trim the ends of the binding strip even with the edges of the quilt. Fold the binding strip all the way over to the back side of the quilt so that the binding does not show on the front of the quilt. Stitch the binding in place by hand. Repeat this step on the opposite edge of the quilt.

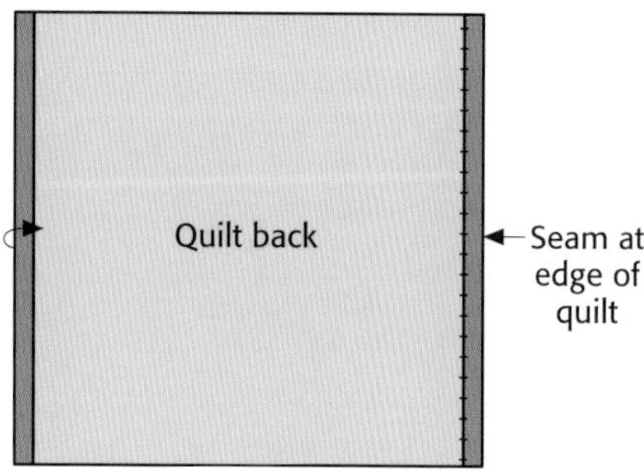

4. Sew the remaining binding strips to the remaining 2 edges of the quilt. Trim the excess fabric in the binding ¼" from the edges of the quilt. Turn under ¼" at each end of the binding, and then fold the binding strips to the back side and stitch them in place.

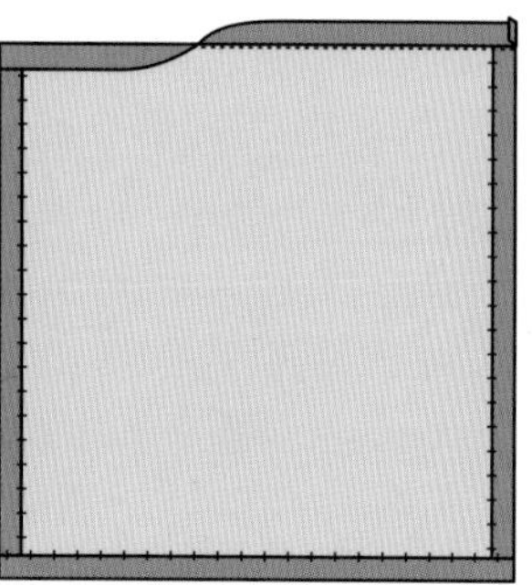

Adding a Hanging Sleeve and Label

THE HANGING SLEEVE described below is wide enough to display a quilt on most types of display rods or poles. The project instructions indicate the width and length to cut each of the strips for the hanging sleeve for that quilt. Follow these steps to prepare and attach the hanging sleeve and label to your quilt.

1. Using a ¼"-wide seam allowance, sew the short ends of the strips together to make one strip long enough for your quilt. Press this seam open.
2. Turn under and sew a ½" hem twice at the short ends of the hanging sleeve. With wrong sides together, sew the long edges together with a ¼" seam allowance. Press this seam open, centering it on the wrong side of the hanging sleeve. Press the long folded edges.
3. Position and pin the hanging sleeve at the top edge of the quilt backing just inside the binding. Appliqué the long edges of the hanging sleeve to the quilt backing.
4. Add a label of your choice to your finished quilt. You can make a label by appliquéing a simple square or rectangle of fabric to the lower right corner of the quilt backing. Another way to create a label is to use one or more of the medium-to-large appliqué shapes from your album blocks as a label. Whatever type of label you decide on, include your name as the quiltmaker, the date you finish the quilt, and any other information you want to record.

Artful ALBUM QUILTS

WAY BEYOND BALTIMORE!

78½" x 78½"

Designed, hand appliquéd, and hand quilted by Jane Townswick, Schnecksville, Pennsylvania, 2000.

My favorite way to select fabrics for an album quilt is what I call the "scrap-liqué" approach. The flowers and birds in this quilt are made from scraps of one-of-a-kind, hand-painted fabrics from Skydyes by Mickey Lawler (see "Resources" on page 125), and I included other scrap fabrics from my stash. The only exception to this is a green Jinny Beyer print I purchased to use in all the blocks and in the border for a sense of unity.

In each of my blocks, I included a small "surprise"—an interruption in pattern or symmetry, or a playful twist on positions of appliqué pieces. For example, one of the flowers in the second block from the left in the top row has eight petals, while all of the others have six. In other blocks, look for flowers with missing center circles or a brown tree with one black branch. See if you can find more fun elements throughout the quilt.

Materials

42"-wide fabric

- 4 yds. off-white for background squares, backing, and hanging sleeve
- Assorted colorful light, medium, and dark scraps for appliqués in blocks and borders and for cornerstones
- 3¾ yds. dark blue tone-on-tone for sashing strips, appliqués in borders, pieced-border corner units, outer border strips, binding, and hanging sleeve
- 2 yds. hand-painted peach-and-orange for pieced inner borders and corner units
- 5¼ yds. for backing and hanging sleeve

Note: *Refer to the quilt photo on facing page and to the block and border patterns on pages 56–124 to determine the sizes of the scraps you'll need for the appliqué shapes in your quilt.*

Cutting

From the off-white fabric, cut:

- 16 squares, each 16" x 16", for backgrounds

From the assorted scrap fabrics, cut:

- The number of appliqué shapes needed for each block and border, referring to the quilt photo on facing page and the pattern pieces on pages 56–124.
- 41 squares, each 2" x 2", for cornerstones in sashing strips and pieced outer border

From the dark blue fabric, cut:

- 40 strips, each 2" x 14½", for sashing
- 32 strips, each 2" x 5", for arrowhead border appliqués
- 16 squares, each 2" x 2", for pieced-border corner units
- 8 strips, each 2" x 14½", for pieced outer border
- 8 strips, each 2" x 22", for pieced outer border
- 8 strips, each 2½" x 42", for binding

From the peach-and-orange fabrics, cut:

- 148 strips, each 2" x 6½", for pieced inner border
- 16 strips, each 2½" x 6½", for pieced inner border

- 8 squares, each 2" x 2", for pieced-border corner units
- 8 strips, each 2" x 3½", for pieced-border corner units
- 8 strips, each 2" x 5" for pieced-border corner units

From the assorted purple fabrics, cut:

- 32 strips, each 2" x 5", for arrowhead border appliqués

From the fabric for backing, cut:

- 2 strips, each 42" x 83", for backing
- 2 strips, each 8½" x 42", for hanging sleeve

Stitching the Blocks

See pages 56–113 for block patterns.

1. Cut and mark the background squares for the 16 blocks in this quilt, referring to "Preparing the Background Fabric" on page 36.
2. Stitch the stems and appliqué shapes in place on the background squares, referring to "Artful Appliqué Techniques" on pages 19–34 and "Stitching Sequences" on page 37.

Assembling the Quilt Center

1. Arrange the blocks in 4 horizontal rows of 4 blocks each. Sew together 5 dark blue sashing strips, each 2" x 14 ½", and 4 blocks to make a horizontal row, starting and ending each row with a sashing strip. Repeat to make a total of 4 horizontal rows.

2. Sew together 5 assorted 2" squares and 4 dark blue sashing strips, each 2" x 14½", to make a horizontal sashing row, starting and ending each row with a 2" square. Repeat to make a total of 5 sashing rows.

3. Sew the sashing rows between the rows of blocks and at the top and bottom edges to complete the quilt center.

Adding the Borders

See page 114 for border pattern.

1. Sew 4 peach strips, each 2" x 6½", to each side of a 2½" x 6½" peach strip to make the 16 border units.

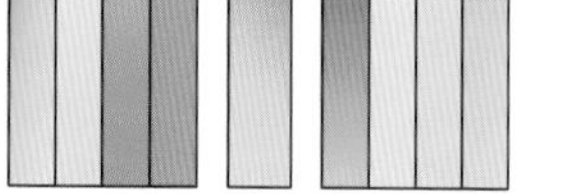

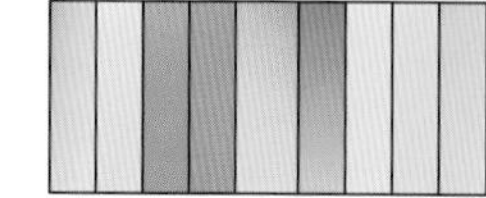

Make 16.

2. Sew 4 border units together with a 2" x 6½" peach strip between them. Add a 2" x 6½" peach strip at each end. Repeat to make 3 more pieced inner borders.

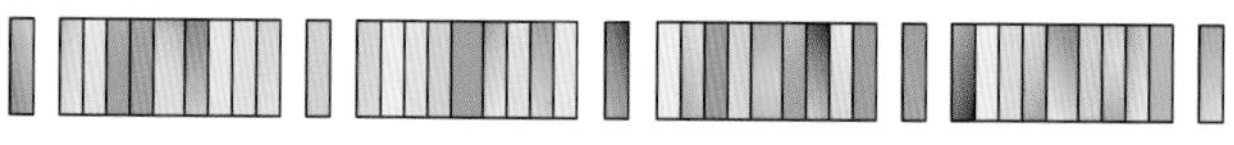

Make 4.

3. Referring to the arrowhead, flower, and leaf patterns on page 114 and "Getting to the Point!" on pages 28–34, stitch the appliqué shapes on each of the 16 border units.

Make 16.

4. Arrange and sew together four 2" dark blue squares, two 2" peach squares, two 2" x 3½" peach rectangles, and two 2" x 5" peach rectangles to make each of 4 pieced corner units.

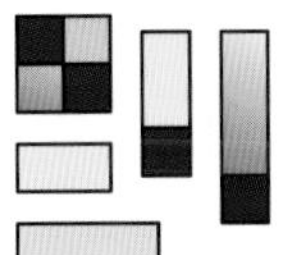

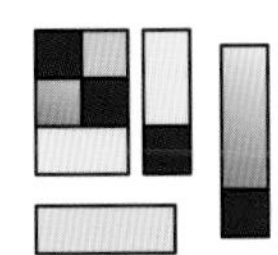

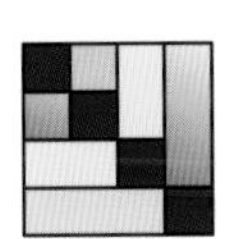

Make 4.

5. Add a pieced corner unit to each end of 2 of the pieced inner borders.

6. Sew the 2 pieced inner borders without corner units to the sides of the quilt top.

7. Sew the remaining 2 pieced inner borders with corner units to the top and bottom edges of the quilt top.

8. Arrange and sew together two 2" x 14½" dark blue strips, 3 assorted 2" squares, and two 2" x 22" dark blue strips to make each of 4 pieced outer borders. Add an additional 2" square to each end of two of the pieced outer borders.

22" 14" 14" 22"

9. Sew the 2 outer borders without corner squares to the sides of the quilt top.

10. Sew the remaining 2 outer borders with corner squares to the top and bottom edges of the quilt top.

Finishing the Quilt

Refer to "Quilting and Finishing" on pages 39–42.

1. Layer the quilt top with batting and backing; baste.
2. Quilt as desired.
3. Bind the edges of the quilt and add a hanging sleeve and a label.

Refer to the quilt photo on page 44 when you sew the corner units to the pieced border. The navy blue squares should go from the corner of the quilt center outward to the quilt corners.

PENNSYLVANIA FLOWER GARDEN

62" x 76"

Designed by Jane Townswick. Machine appliquéd by Gail Kessler, Oley, Pennsylvania, 2000. Machine quilted by Carol Singer.

The colors of the appliqués in this quilt are luminous against the dark walnut background. Because the colors are so saturated and vibrant, they would also look great on a light background. Gail glue-basted under the seam allowance of each appliqué and did a tiny blanket stitch on her new Bernina 180E sewing machine, using a very fine (size 60) needle and YLI's Wonder Invisible thread in the top and bobbin. The result is a magnificent album quilt that is as much fun to make as it is to admire. For information about ordering a fabric kit for this quilt top, see "Resources" on page 125.

Materials

42"-wide fabric

- 5 yds. dark walnut for block and border backgrounds
- Assorted scraps of colorful lights, mediums, and darks for appliqués in blocks and borders
- 5 yds. for backing, binding, and hanging sleeve

NOTE: *Refer to the quilt photo on facing page and to the block and border patterns on pages 56–124 to determine the sizes of the scraps you'll need for the appliqué shapes in your quilt.*

Cutting

From the dark walnut fabric, cut:

- 12 squares, each 16" x 16", for block backgrounds
- 2 strips, each 11½" x 78", for side borders
- 2 strips, each 11½" x 64", for top and bottom borders

From the assorted scrap fabrics, cut:

- The number of appliqué shapes needed for the quilt blocks and borders, referring to the quilt photo on facing page and the pattern pieces on pages 56–124.

From the fabric for backing, cut:

- 2 strips, each 40" x 66", for backing
- 7 strips, each 2½" x 42", for binding
- 2 strips, each 8½" x 42", for hanging sleeve

Stitching the Blocks

See pages 56–113 for block patterns.

1. Cut and mark the background squares for the 12 blocks in this quilt, referring to "Preparing the Background Fabric" on page 36.
2. Stitch the stems and appliqué shapes in place on the background squares, referring to "Artful Appliqué Techniques" on pages 19–34 and "Stitching Sequences" on page 37.

Assembling the Quilt Center

Arrange the blocks in 4 horizontal rows of 3 blocks each. Sew the blocks together in horizontal rows. Join the rows to complete the quilt center.

Adding the Borders

See pages 115–118 for border patterns.

1. Stitch the appliqué shapes on the border strips, waiting to stitch the corner appliqués until after you stitch the border strips to the quilt center. Press the partially appliquéd border strips, referring to "Pressing and Trimming" on page 37.
2. Trim the top and bottom border strips to 10½" x 64" and trim the side border strips to 10½" x 78", referring to "Pressing and Trimming" on page 37 and to the center marks indicated on the patterns.
3. Measure your quilt center from top to bottom and from side to side through the center.
4. Fold the top and bottom border strips in half and mark each of the centers with a pin. Mark half the measurement of the quilt center with a pin near each end of each border strip.

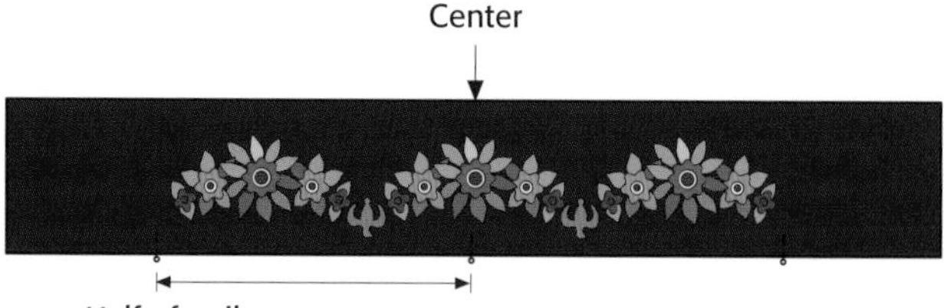

5. Fold each side of the quilt center in half and mark the center with a pin. Pin the top and bottom border strips to the top and bottom edges of the quilt, matching the center pins and the outer pins on the border strip to the edges of the quilt center.
6. Sew the top and bottom border strips onto the top and bottom edges of your quilt center, beginning and ending the seams ¼" in from each corner. Backstitch to secure ends of the seams.
7. Stitch the side border strips to your quilt center in the same manner, beginning and ending the seams ¼" in from the corners.
8. Fold 2 adjacent border strips at a 45° angle, creating the corner fold. Lightly press the fold in place. Open the border strips and pin the corner appliqué motifs in position. Appliqué the corner shapes, checking your work periodically and making slight adjustments if necessary. Appliqué to about 2" from the corner fold. Repeat at the remaining 3 corners of the quilt top.
9. Turn under the border strips, as before, to check the accuracy of the mitered corner folds, and press them. Place the border strips right sides together and sew the mitered corner seams, working from the outer corner toward the quilt center. Trim these seam allowances to ¼" and press them open. Stitch

the final corner appliqués in place over the mitered seams, adjusting the positions of the shapes slightly if necessary. Press the stitched border corners.

10. Repeat steps 8 and 9 for mitering the 3 remaining corners.

Finishing the Quilt

Refer to "Quilting and Finishing" on pages 39–42.

1. Layer the quilt top with batting and backing; baste.
2. Quilt as desired.
3. Bind the edges of the quilt and add a hanging sleeve and a label.

RHAPSODY IN RED AND BLACK

64" x 64"

Designed by Jane Townswick. Hand appliquéd by Seta Wehbe, Newtown Square, Pennsylvania, 2000. Machine quilted by Teresa Fusco.

Each block in this quilt features one fabric that is unique to that block (see if you can find the antique print in the block at the upper left corner). Within each block, Seta repeated fabrics three times each to create a visual balance. She also featured the patterns in various prints creatively within her appliqué shapes, so that no two flowers would look identical, even when made from the same fabric. There are no birds in any of the blocks in this quilt, which creates a contemporary look. A wide range of values, from the deep, dark sashing strips to bright flowers and very light leaves, makes Seta's quilt sparkle with energy.

Materials

42"-wide fabric

- 3 yds. total assorted neutral prints for block and middle border backgrounds
- Assorted scraps of colorful lights, mediums, and darks for appliqués in blocks and middle border
- 3½ yds. black tone-on-tone for sashing strips, inner border, middle border, outer border, and binding
- 1½ yds. red-and-black stripe for middle border
- 4½ yds. for backing and hanging sleeve

NOTE: *Refer to the quilt photo on facing page and to the block and border patterns on pages 56–124 to determine the sizes of the scraps you'll need for the appliqué shapes in your quilt.*

Cutting

From the assorted neutral prints, cut:

- 9 squares, each 16" x 16", for block backgrounds
- 4 strips, each 7" x 16", for middle border backgrounds

From the assorted colorful fabrics, cut:

- The number of appliqué shapes needed for each block, referring to the quilt photo on facing page and the pattern pieces on pages 56–124.

From the black print, cut the following along the crosswise grain:

- 8 strips, each 2½" x 5½", for middle border
- 8 strips, each 2½" x 42", for "no-binding" binding

From the black print, cut the following along the lengthwise grain:

- 6 strips, each 2½" x 14½", for horizontal sashing strips
- 2 strips, each 2½" x 46½", for vertical sashing strips
- 4 strips, each 2½" x 52", for inner border
- 4 strips, each 2½" x 66", for outer border

From the red-and-black stripe, cut:

- 8 strips, each 5½" x 23", for middle border

From the fabric for backing, cut:

- 2 strips, each 34" x 68", for backing
- 2 strips, each 8½" x 42", for hanging sleeve

Stitching the Blocks

See pages 56–113 for block patterns.

1. Cut and mark the background squares for the 9 blocks in this quilt, referring to "Preparing the Background Fabric" on page 36.
2. Stitch the stems and appliqué shapes in place on the background squares, referring to "Artful Appliqué Techniques" on pages 19–34, and "Stitching Sequences" on page 37.

Assembling the Quilt Center

Arrange the blocks in 3 rows of 3 blocks each. Sew together three blocks and two 2½" x 14½" black sashing strips in horizontal rows. Repeat to make 2 more horizontal rows of blocks. Sew the rows together with 2½" x 46½" sashing strips between them.

Adding the Borders

See pages 119–124 for border patterns.

1. Fold each of the 2½" x 52" inner border strips and the 2½" x 66" outer border strips in half and mark each of the centers with a pin. Set these aside for now.
2. Referring to the quilt photo on page 52 and the pattern pieces on pages 119–124, stitch the border appliqués in place on the four 7" x 16" middle border strips. Press and trim these strips to 5½" x 14½", referring to "Pressing and Trimming" on page 37 and to the center marks indicated on the patterns.
3. Sew a 2½" x 5½" black strip to each short end of the 5½" x 14½" border appliqué strips. Sew a 5½" x 23" red-and-black strip to the short ends of each of these border appliqué strips to complete the middle borders. Fold each middle border strip in half and mark the centers with a pin.

Make 4.

4. Sew together an inner border, a middle border, and an outer border, matching the center pins. Repeat to make 3 more of these borders.

Make 4.

5. Sew the borders to the quilt top, referring to directions for mitering corners on page 50, steps 3–10.

Finishing the Quilt

Refer to "Quilting and Finishing" on pages 39–42.

1. Layer the quilt top with batting and backing; baste.
2. Quilt as desired.
3. Bind the edges of the quilt and add a hanging sleeve and a label.

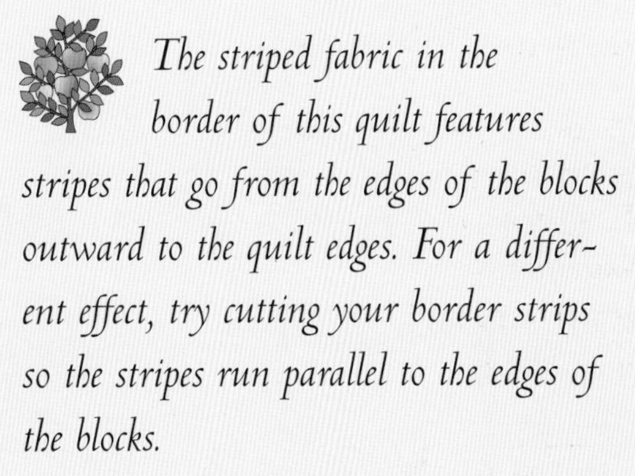

The striped fabric in the border of this quilt features stripes that go from the edges of the blocks outward to the quilt edges. For a different effect, try cutting your border strips so the stripes run parallel to the edges of the blocks.

Scalloped Tulip Wreath

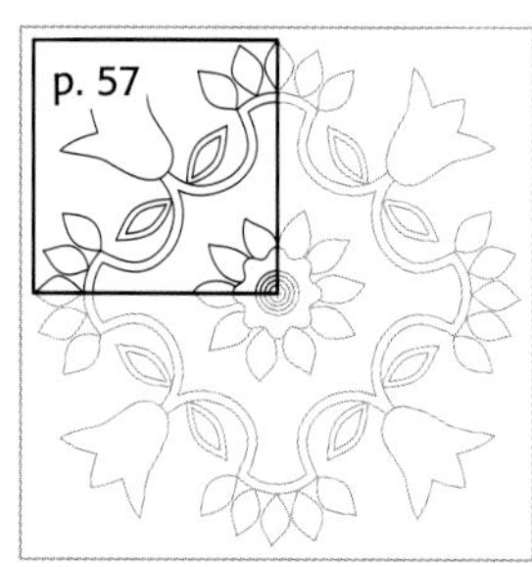

Flip pattern along this line.
Flip pattern along this line.
Center

Friendship Flowers

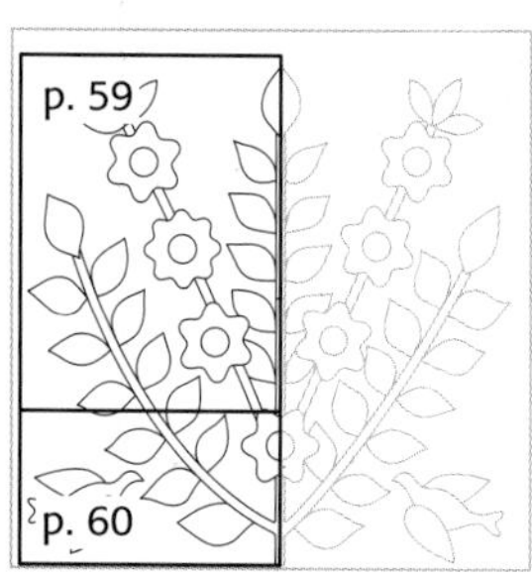

p. 60
Flip pattern along this line.
Center
Connect to pattern on page 60.

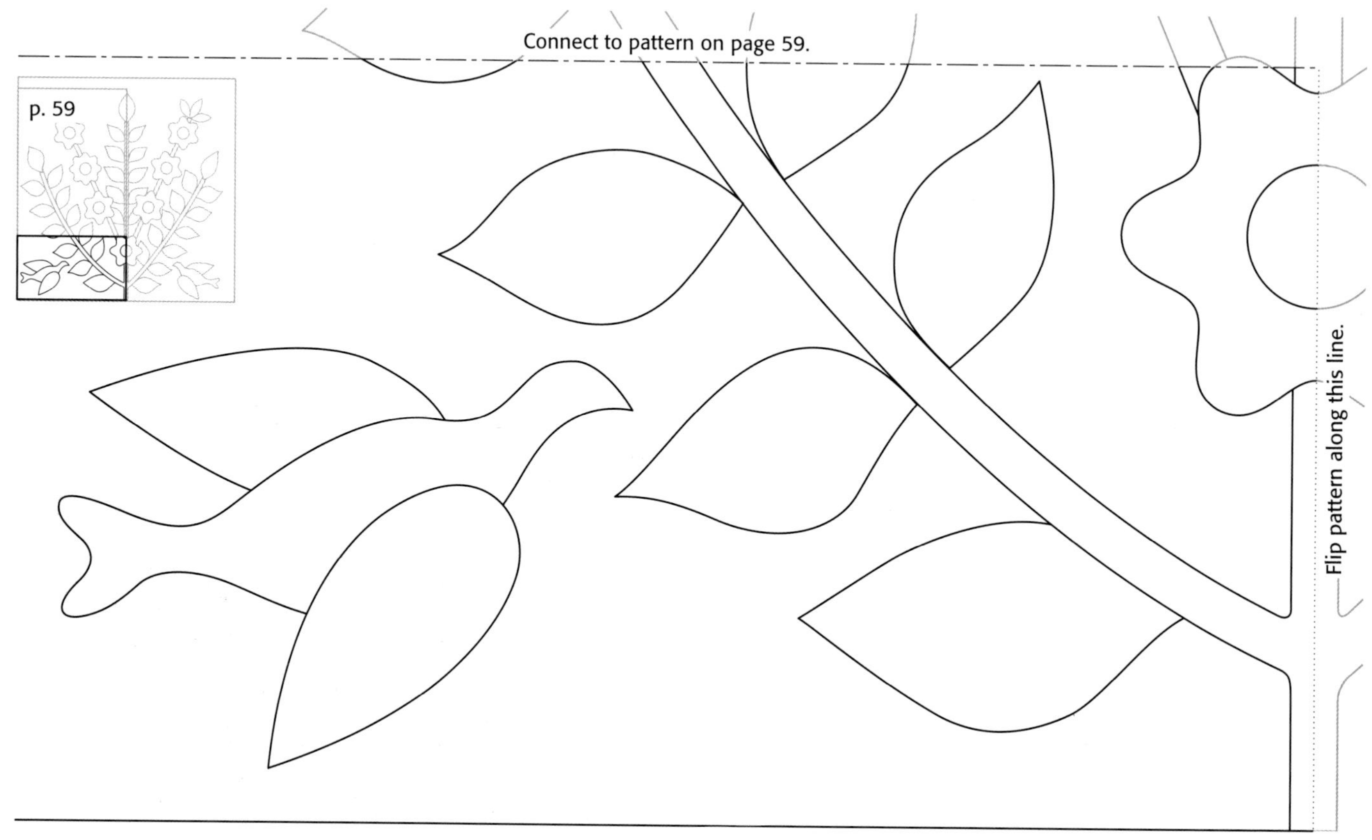
Connect to pattern on page 59.
p. 59
Flip pattern along this line.

Crimson Blossoms

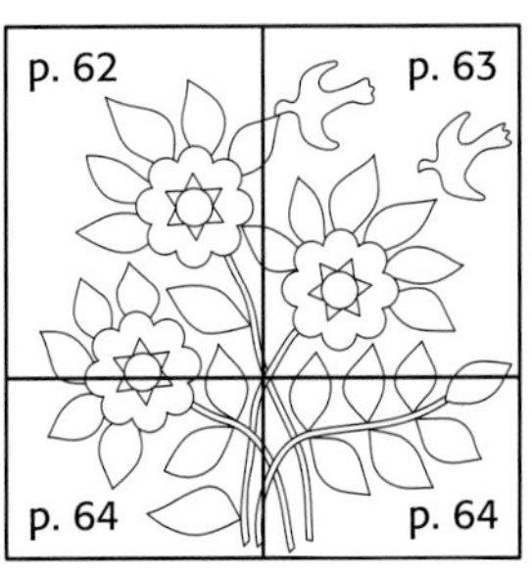

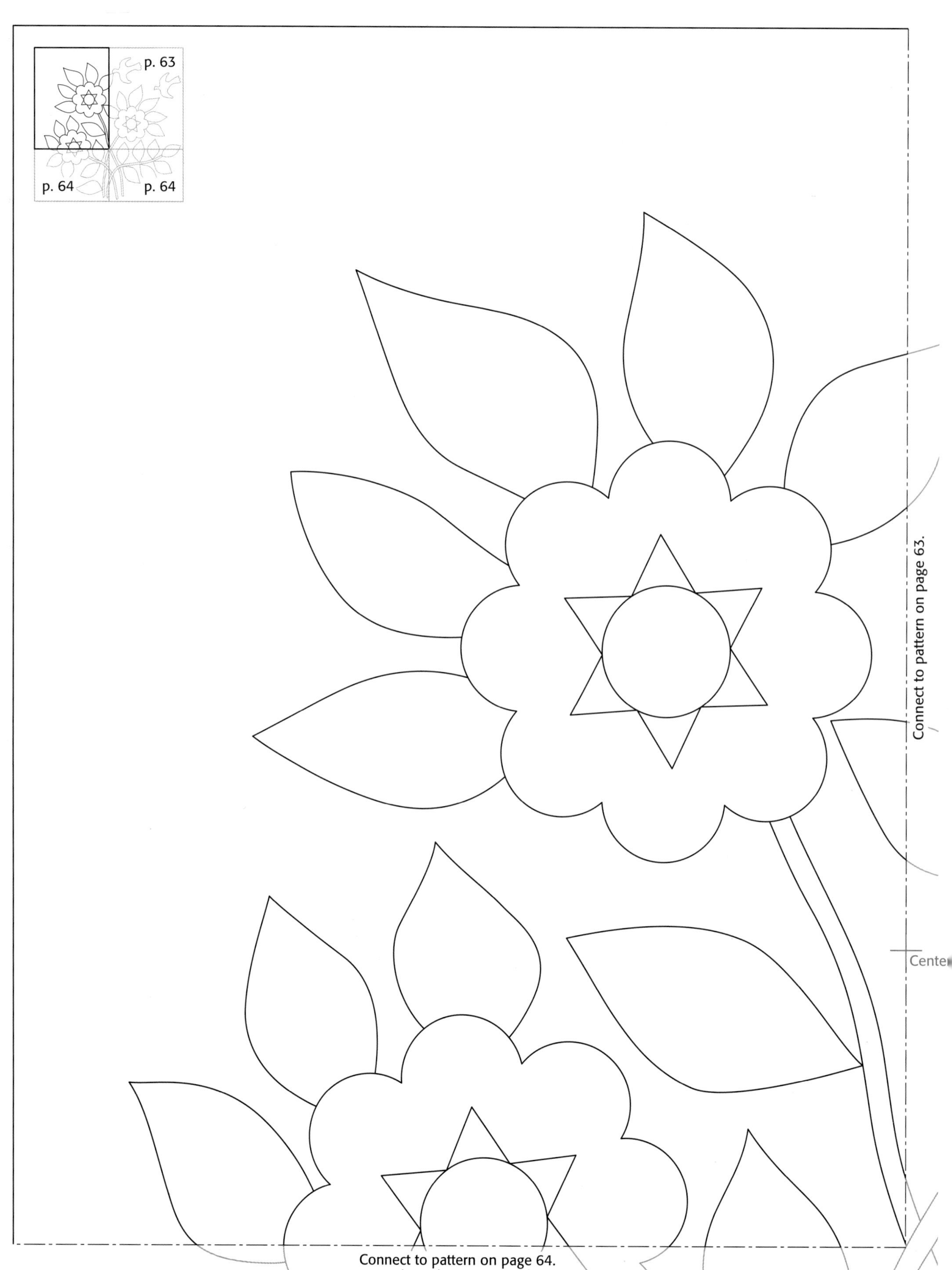

Connect to pattern on page 64.

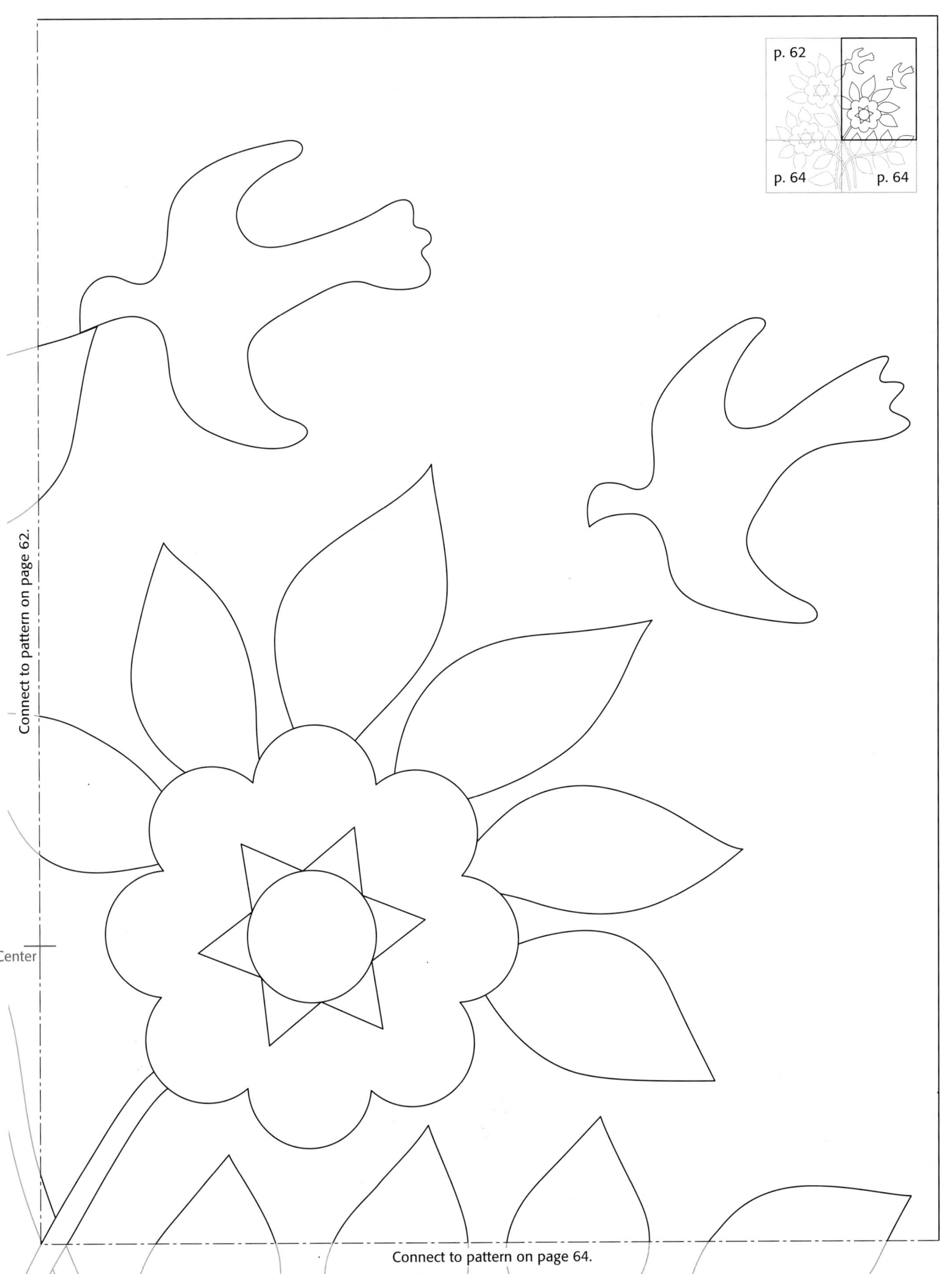
p. 62
p. 64
p. 64
Connect to pattern on page 62.
Center
Connect to pattern on page 64.

Connect to pattern on page 62.

Connect to pattern at bottom of page.

p. 62 p. 63

p. 64

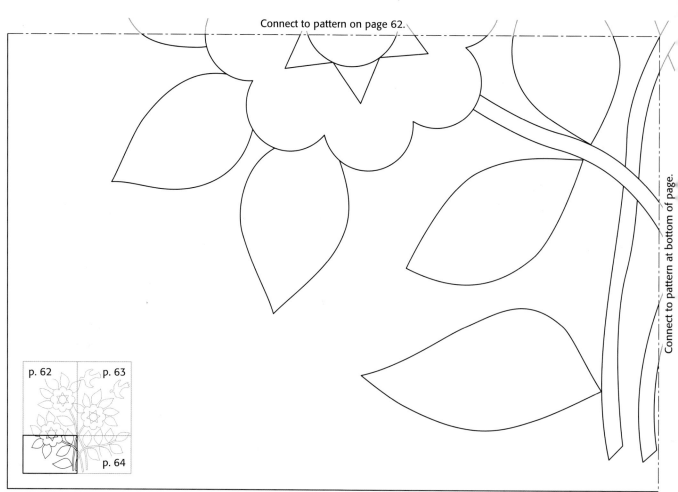

Connect to pattern on page 63.

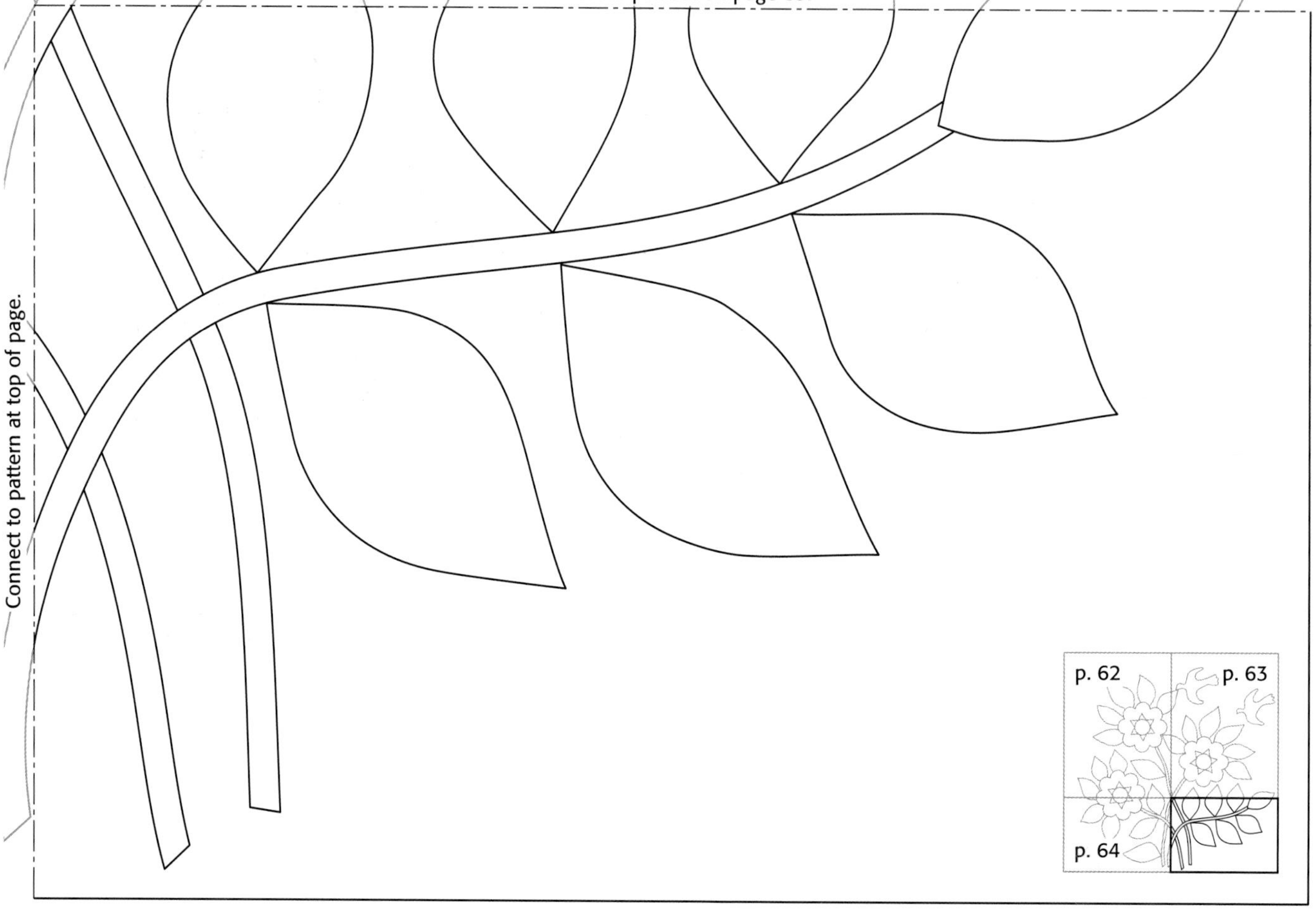

Connect to pattern at top of page.

p. 62 p. 63

p. 64

Circle of Teardrops

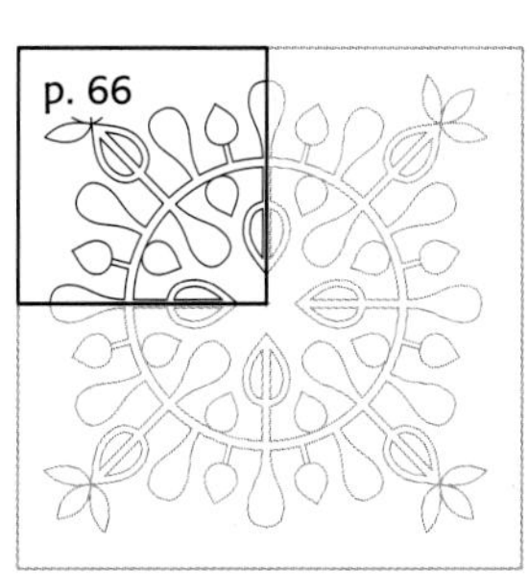

Flip pattern along this line.

Flip pattern along this line.

Center

Peach Tree

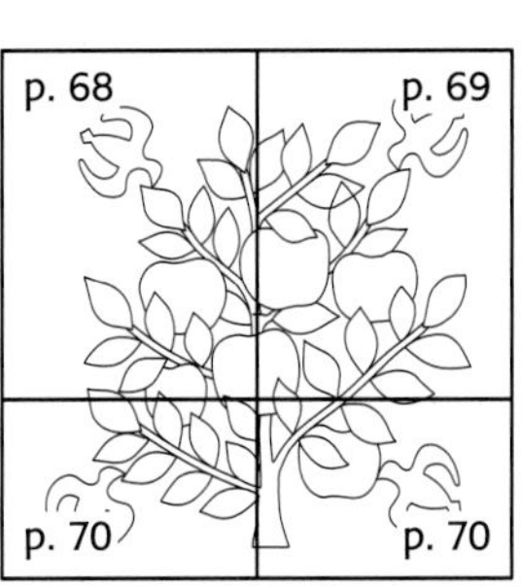

p. 69
p. 70
p. 70
Connect to pattern on page 69.
Center
Connect to pattern on page 70.

p. 68
p. 70
p. 70
Connect to pattern on page 68.
Center
Connect to pattern on page 70.

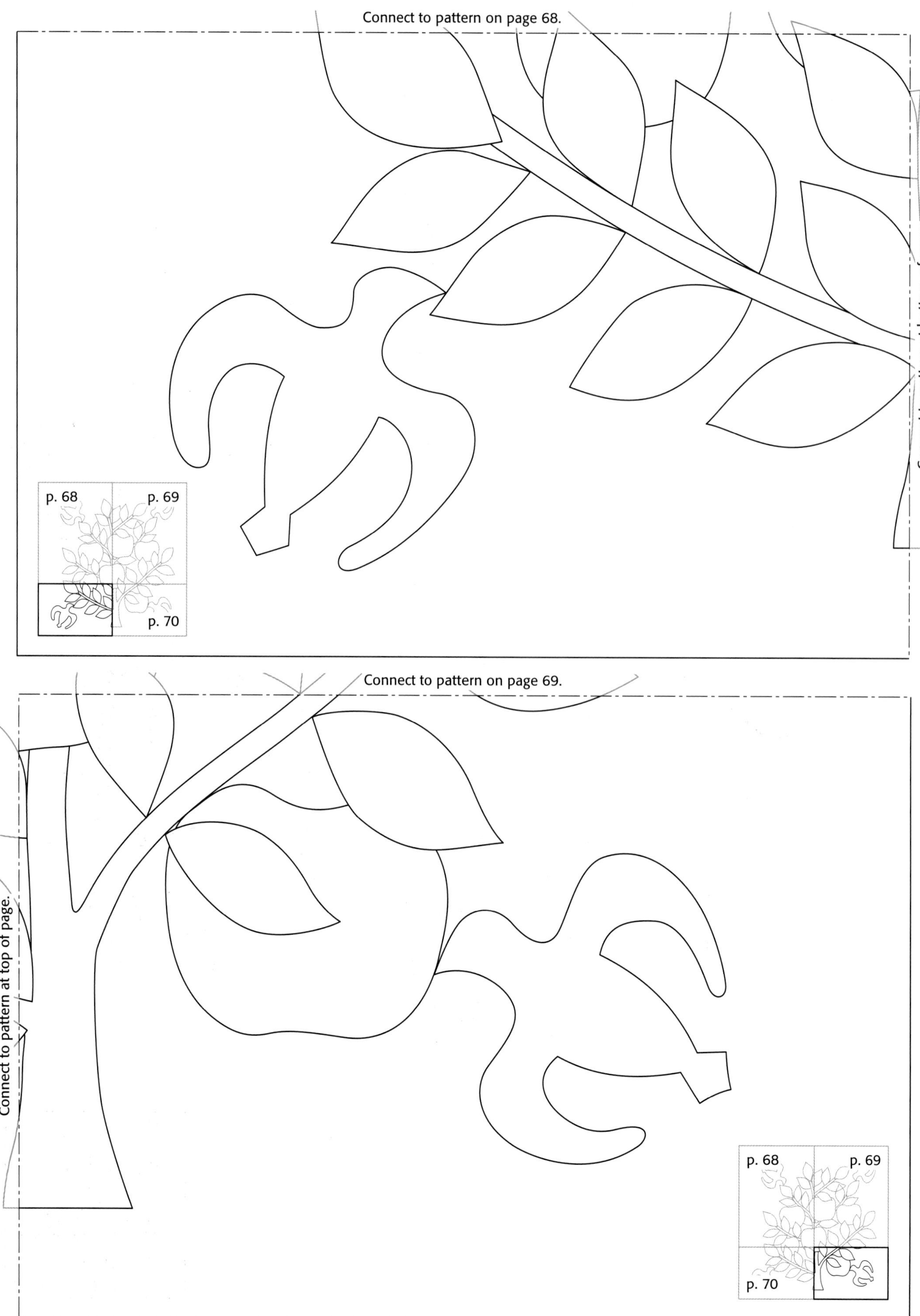
Connect to pattern on page 68.
Connect to pattern at bottom of page.
p. 68
p. 69
p. 70
Connect to pattern on page 69.
Connect to pattern at top of page.
p. 68
p. 69
p. 70

Mirror Images

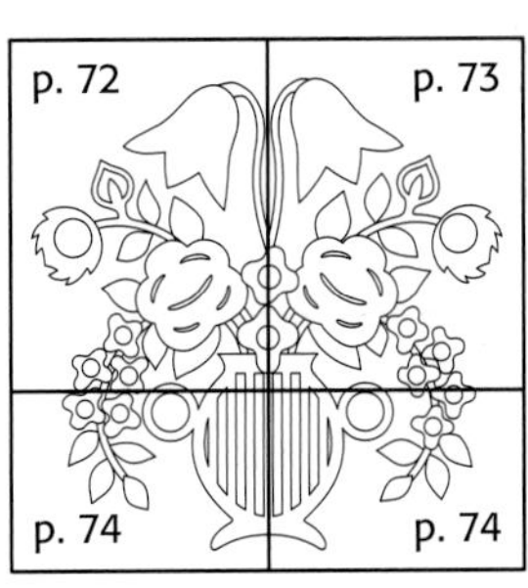

p. 73
p. 74
p. 74
Connect to pattern on page 73.
Center
Connect to pattern on page 74.

Connect to pattern on page 72.

Connect to pattern on page 74.

Connect to pattern on page 72.
Connect to pattern at bottom of page.
p. 72
p. 73
p. 74
Connect to pattern on page 73.
Connect to pattern at top of page.
p. 72
p. 73
p. 74

Vintage Vase

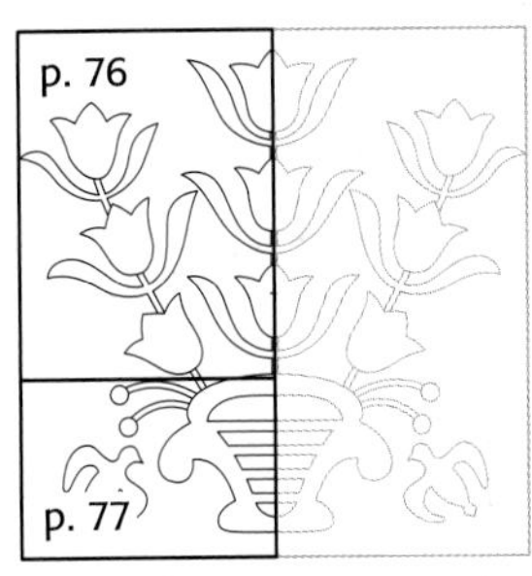

p. 77
Flip pattern along this line.
Center
Connect to pattern on page 77.

Connect to pattern on page 76.
p. 76
Flip pattern along this line.

Tree of Life

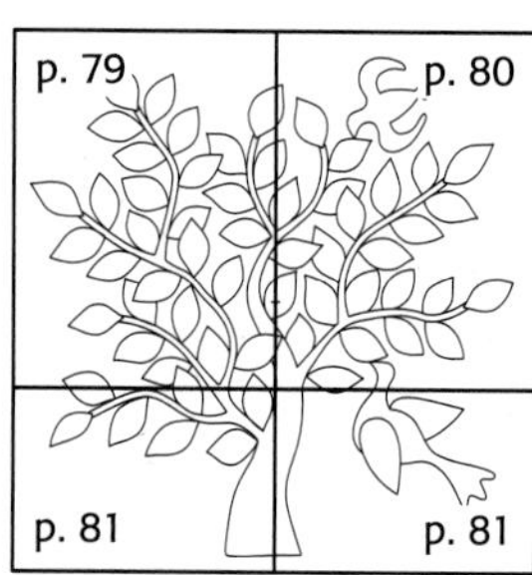

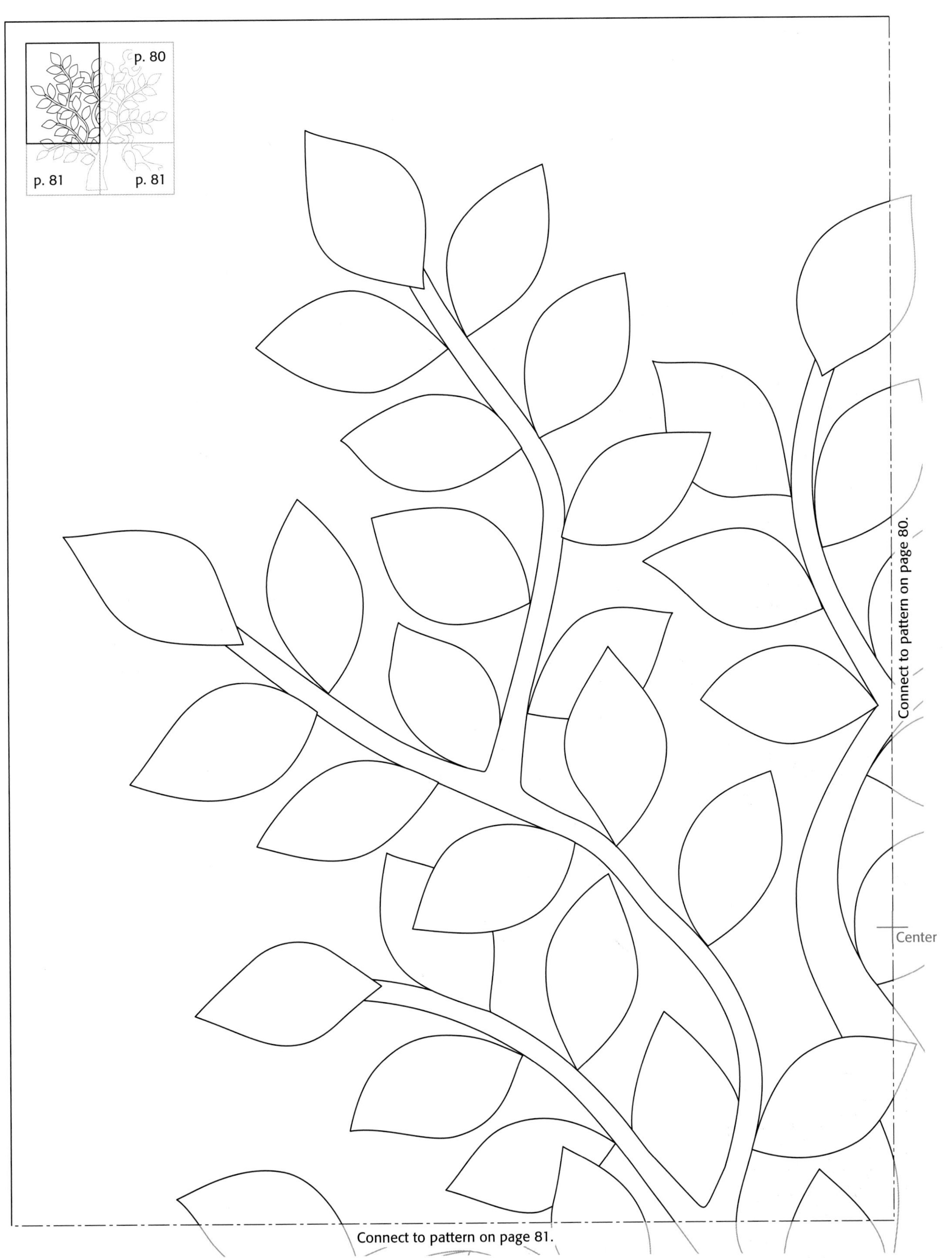
p. 80
p. 81
p. 81
Connect to pattern on page 80.
Center
Connect to pattern on page 81.

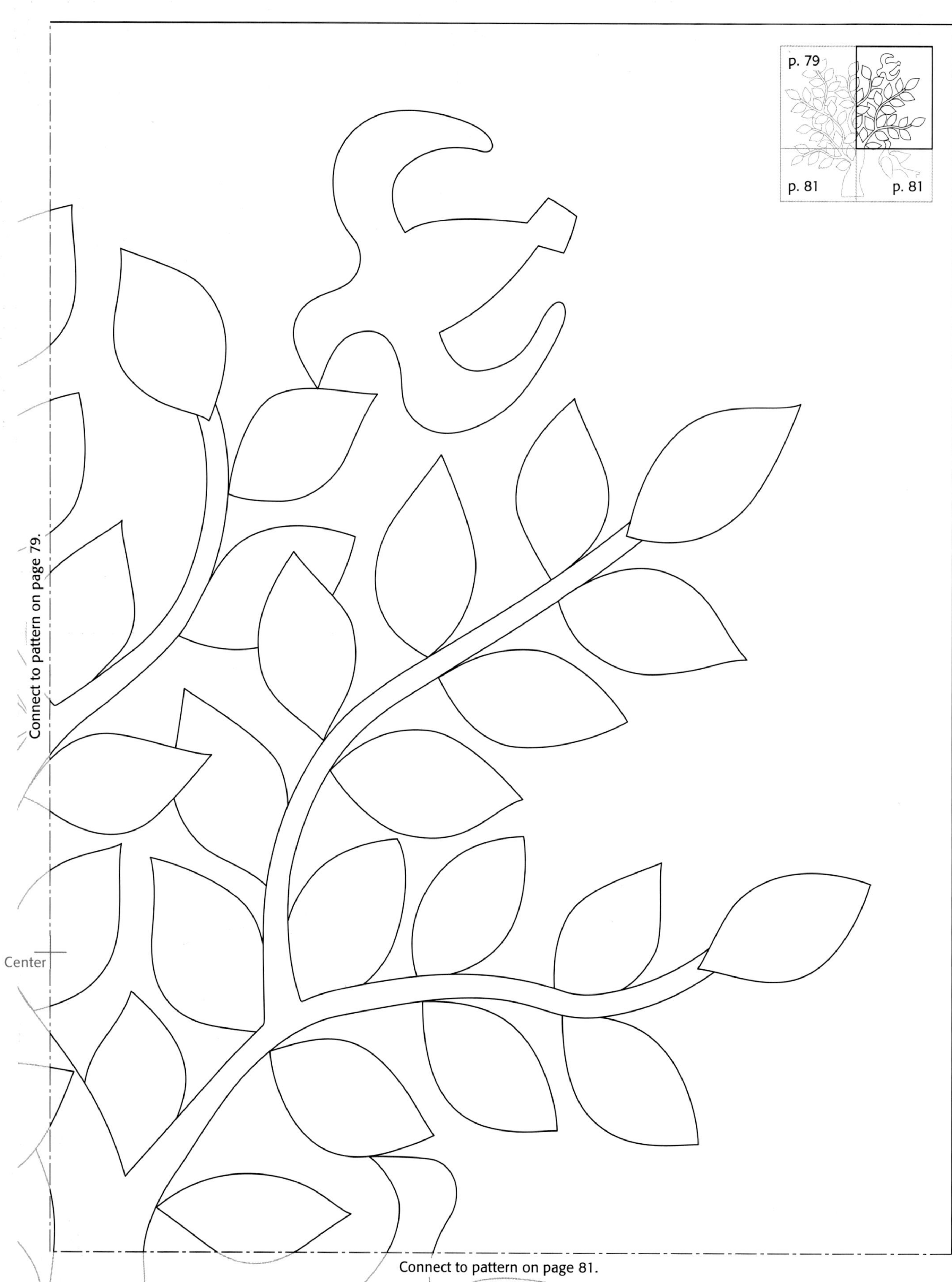
p. 79
p. 81
p. 81
Connect to pattern on page 79.
Center
Connect to pattern on page 81.

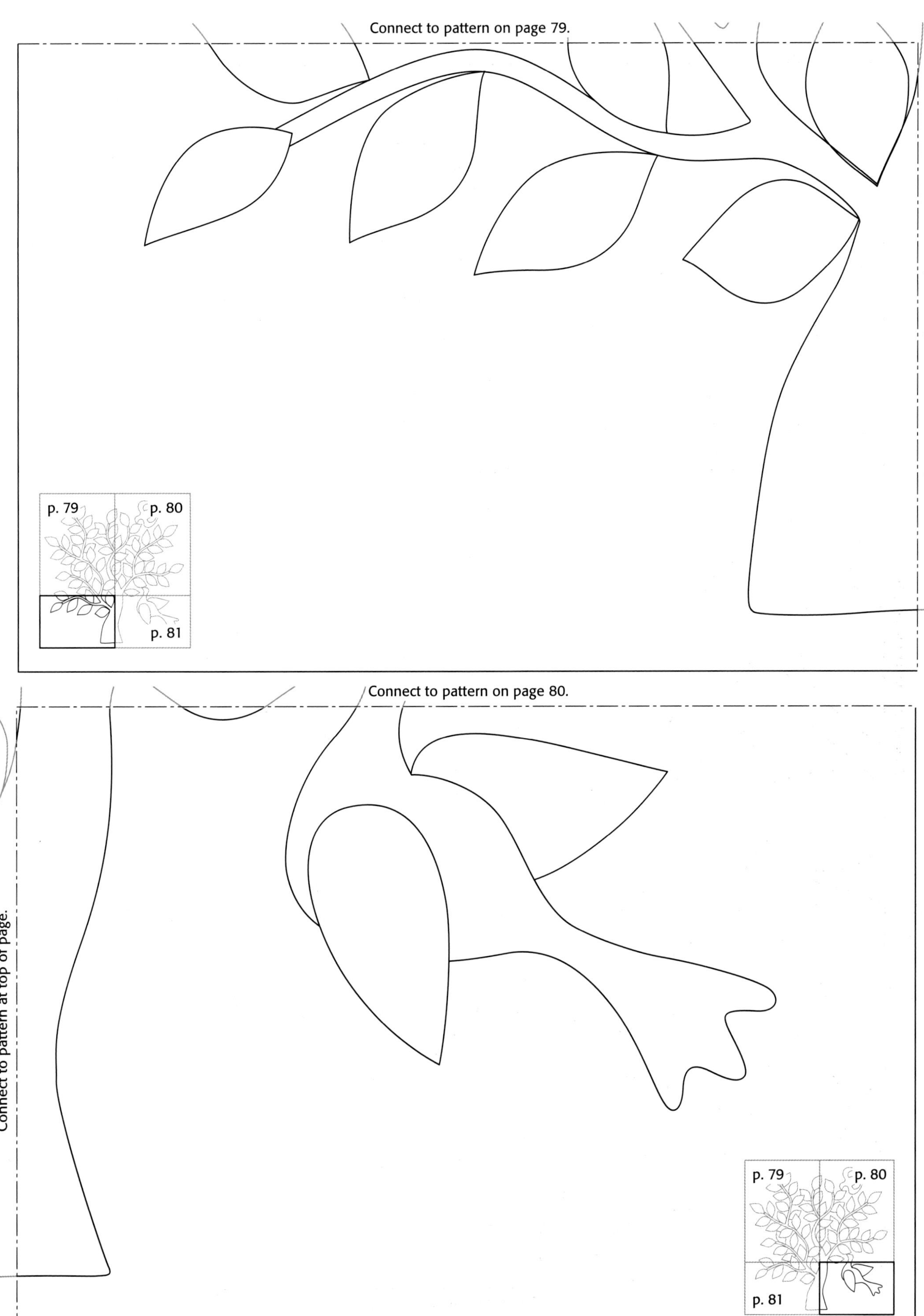
Connect to pattern on page 79.
Connect to pattern at bottom of page.
p. 79
p. 80
p. 81
Connect to pattern on page 80.
Connect to pattern at top of page.
p. 79
p. 80
p. 81

Spring Tulips

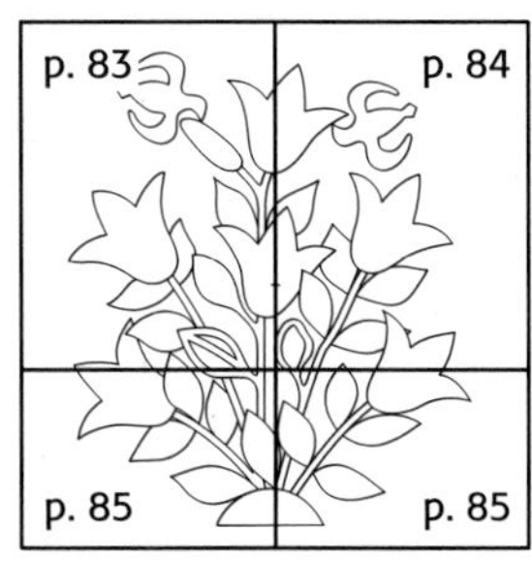

p. 84
p. 85
p. 85
Connect to pattern on page 84.
Center
Connect to pattern on page 85.

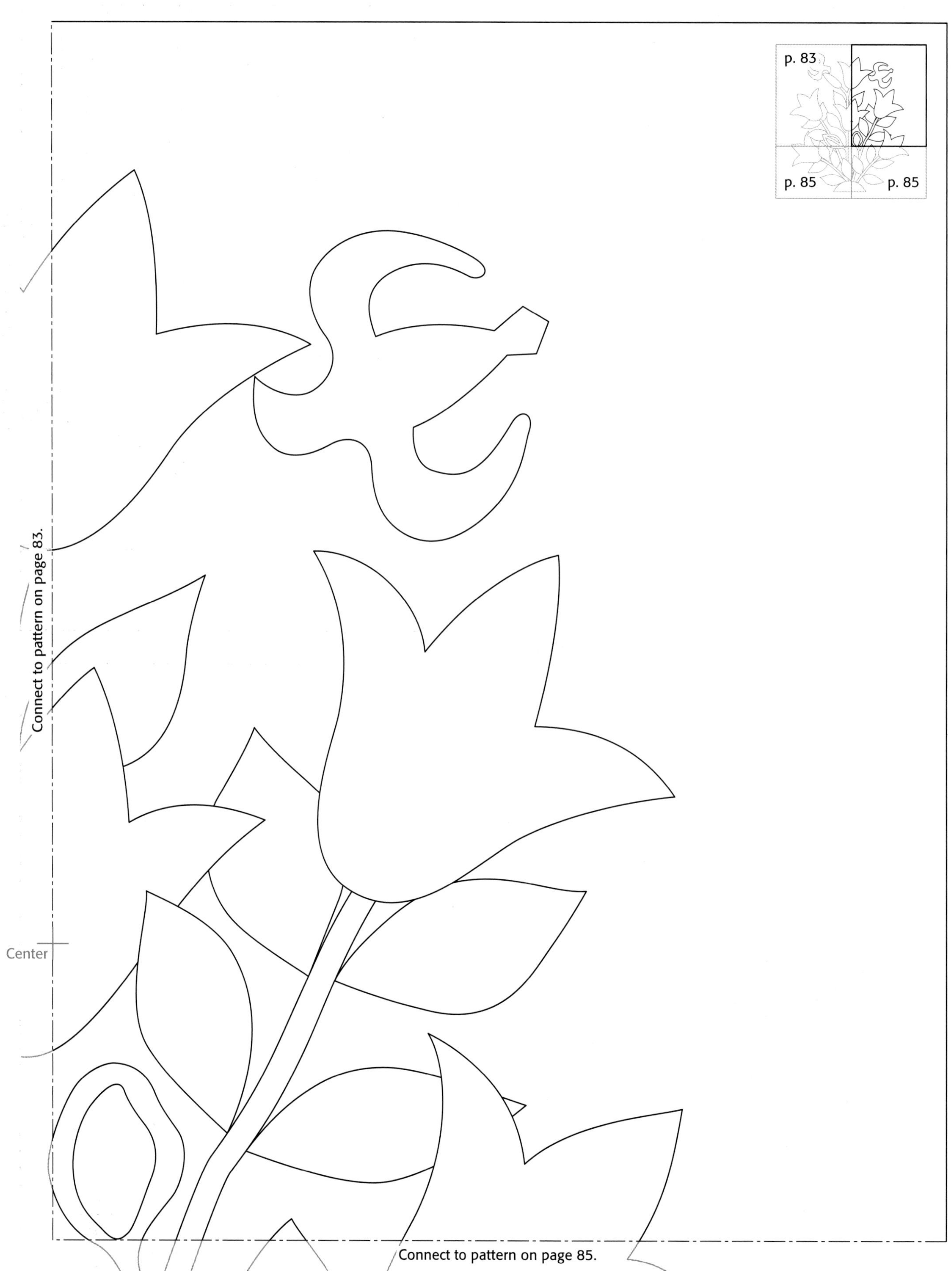
p. 83
p. 85
p. 85
Connect to pattern on page 83.
Center
Connect to pattern on page 85.

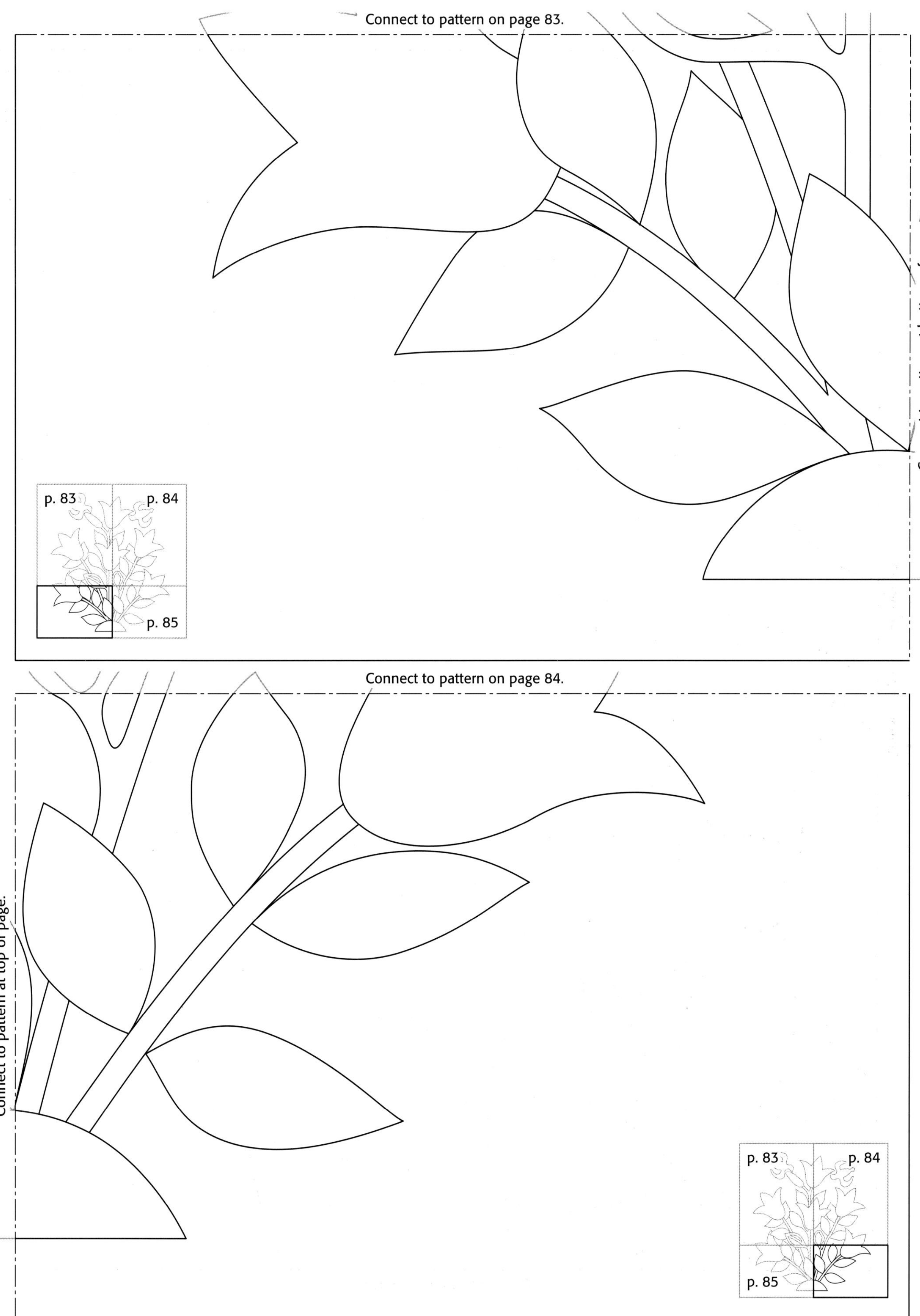

Connect to pattern on page 83.
Connect to pattern at bottom of page.
p. 83
p. 84
p. 85
Connect to pattern on page 84.
Connect to pattern at top of page.
p. 83
p. 84
p. 85

Blooming Cactus

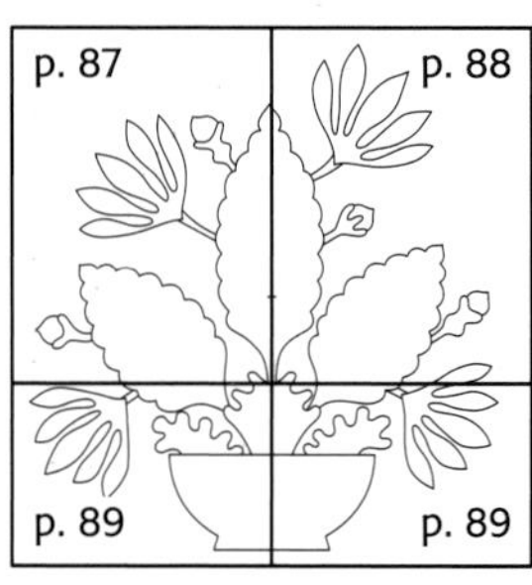

p. 88
p. 89
p. 89
Connect to pattern on page 88.
Center
Connect to pattern on page 89.

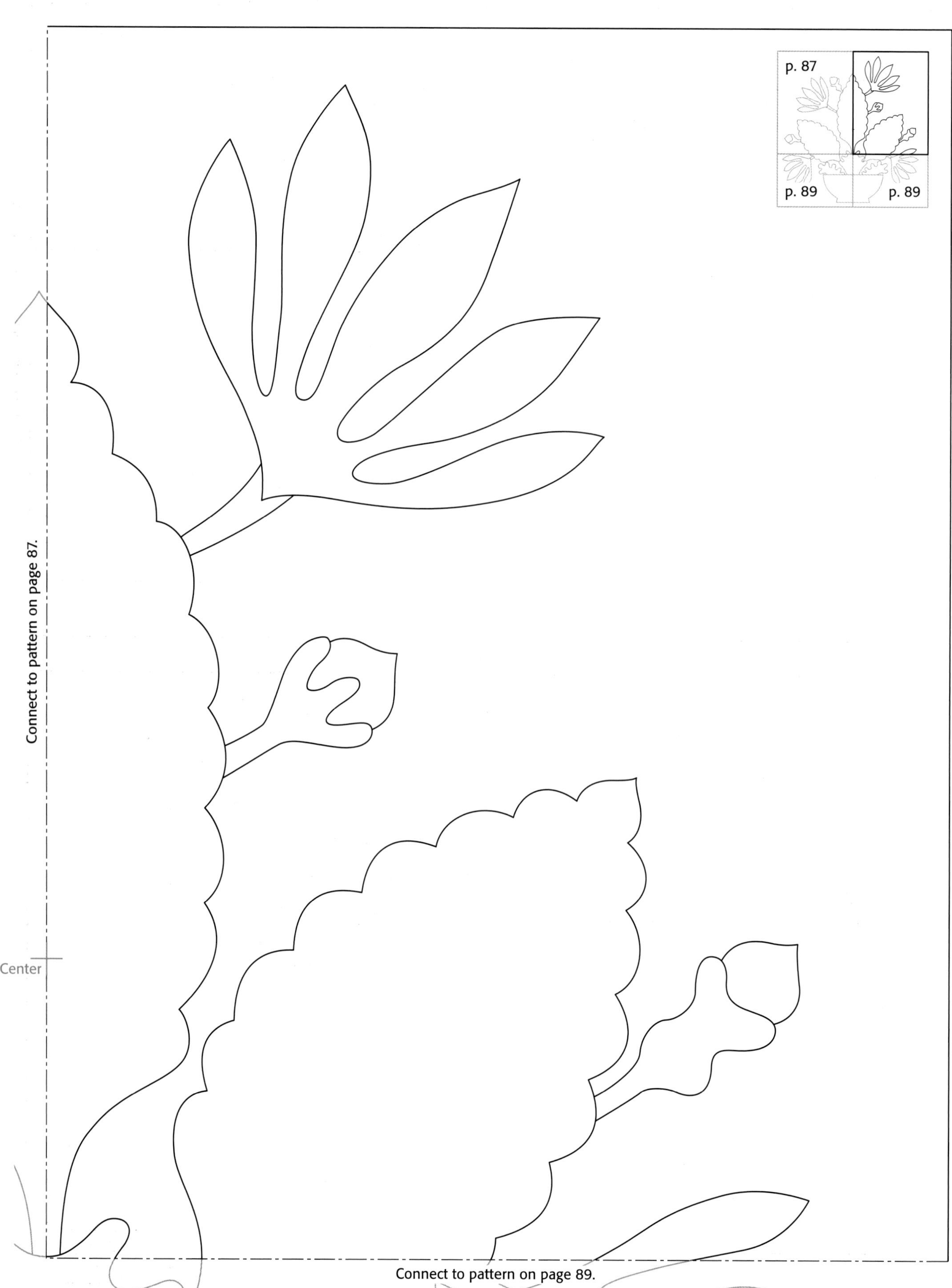
p. 87
p. 89
p. 89
Connect to pattern on page 87.
Center
Connect to pattern on page 89.

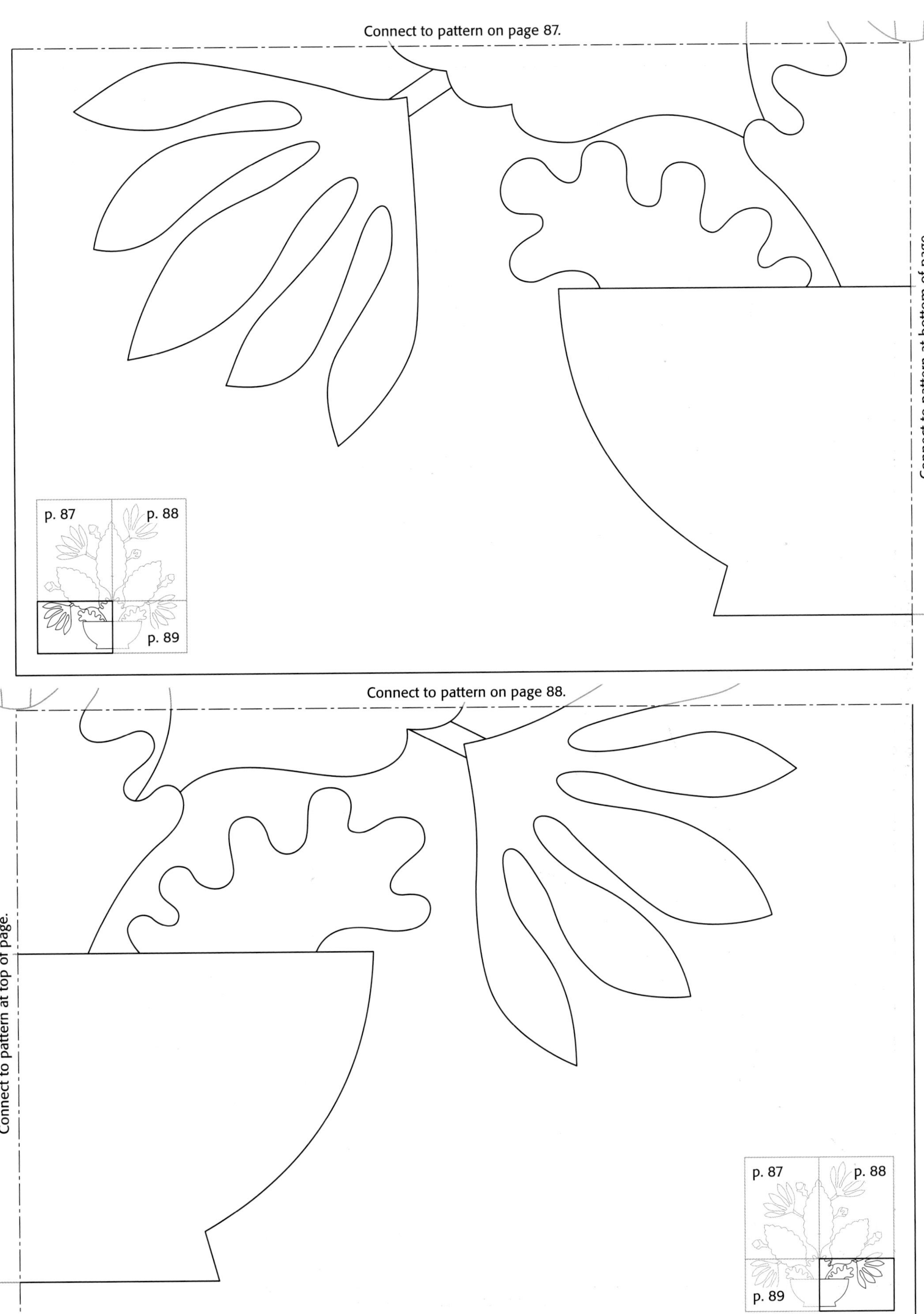
Connect to pattern on page 87.
Connect to pattern at bottom of page.
p. 87
p. 88
p. 89
Connect to pattern on page 88.
Connect to pattern at top of page.
p. 87
p. 88
p. 89

Beyond Baltimore

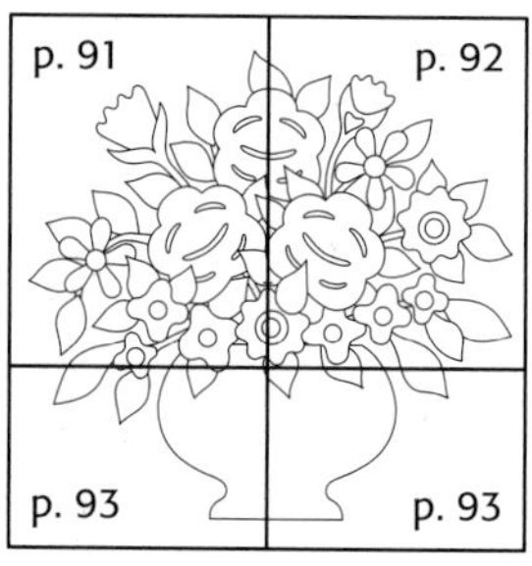

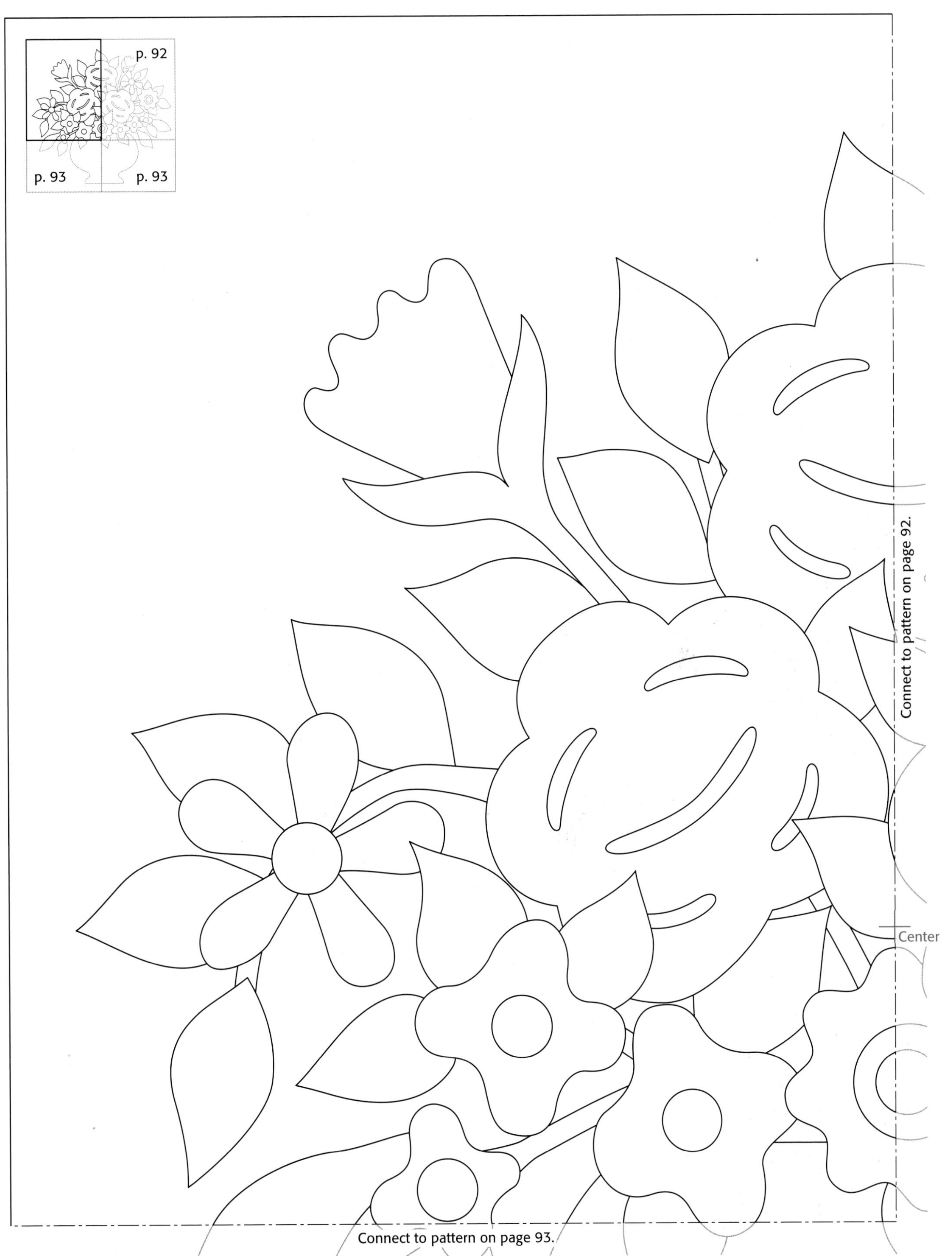
p. 92
p. 93
p. 93
Connect to pattern on page 92.
Center
Connect to pattern on page 93.

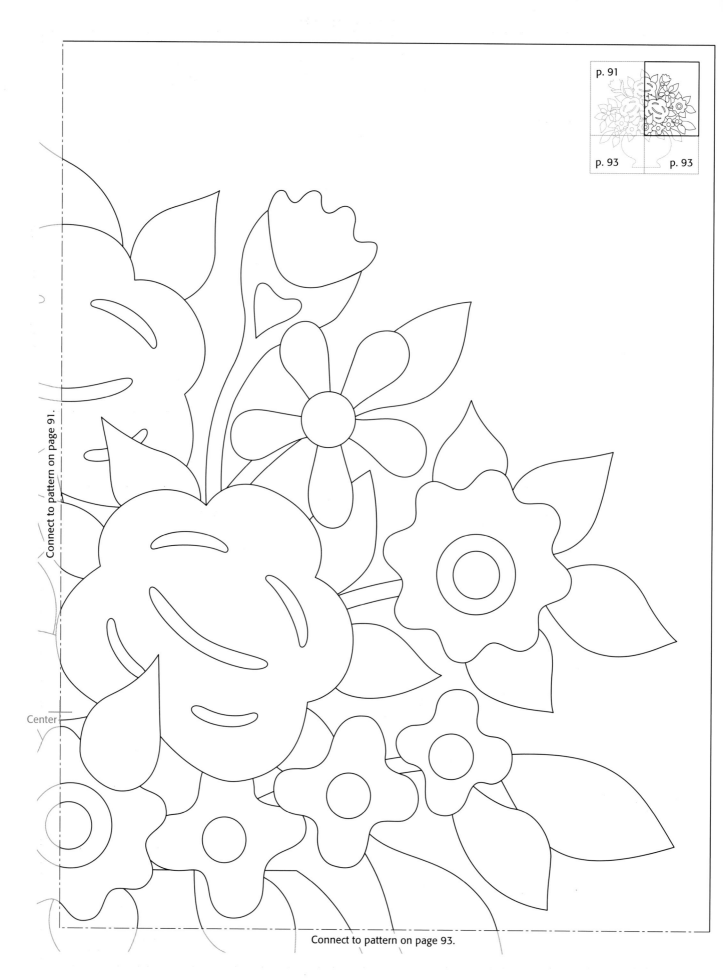
p. 91
p. 93
p. 93
Connect to pattern on page 91.
Center
Connect to pattern on page 93.

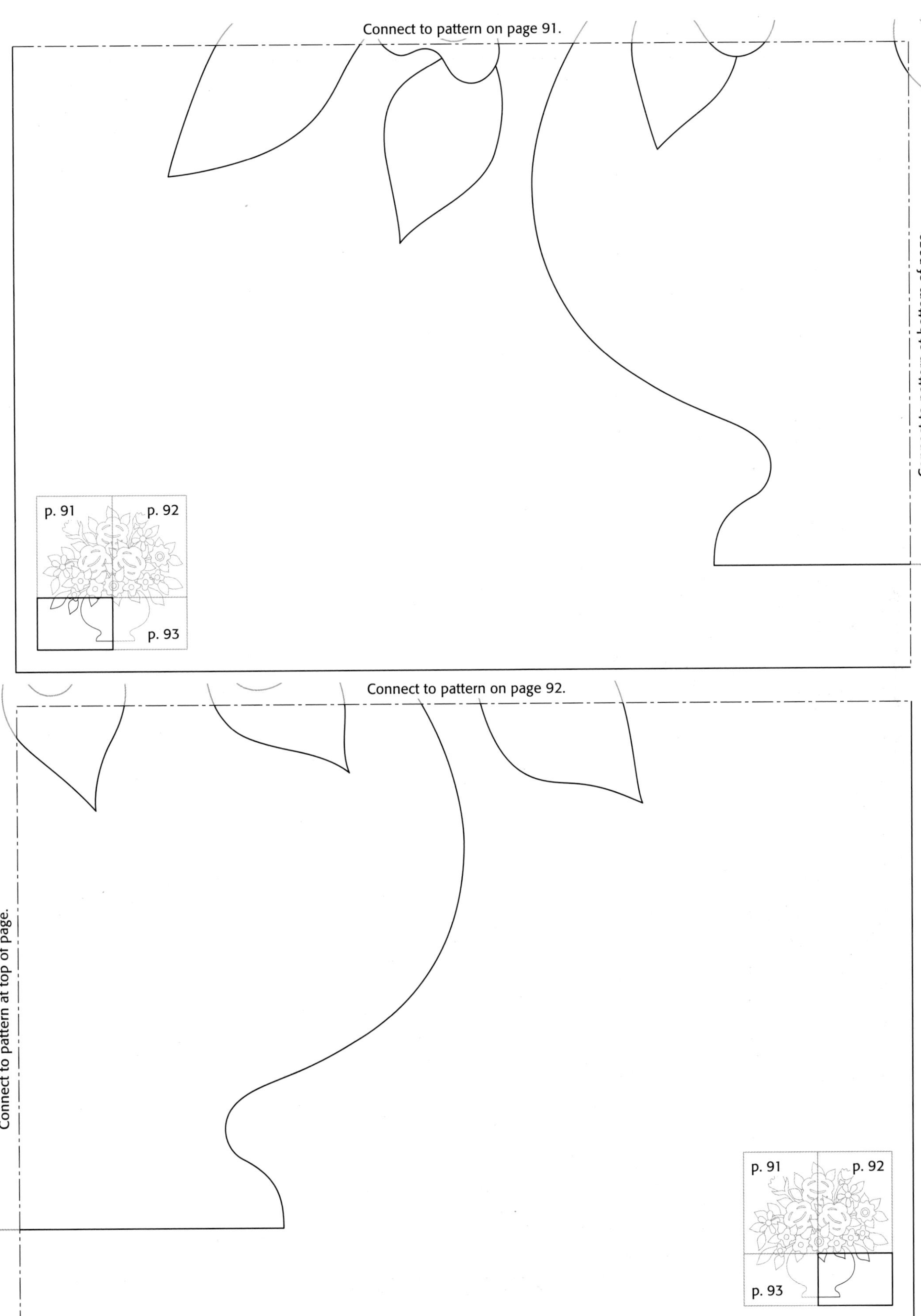

Connect to pattern on page 91.
Connect to pattern at bottom of page.
p. 91
p. 92
p. 93
Connect to pattern on page 92.
Connect to pattern at top of page.
p. 91
p. 92
p. 93

Folk Art Bouquet

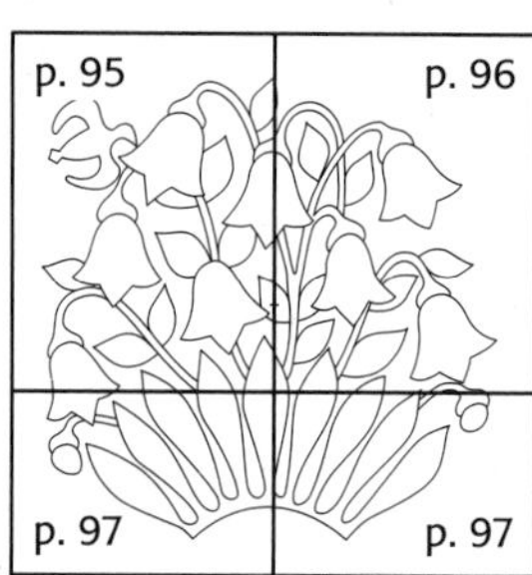

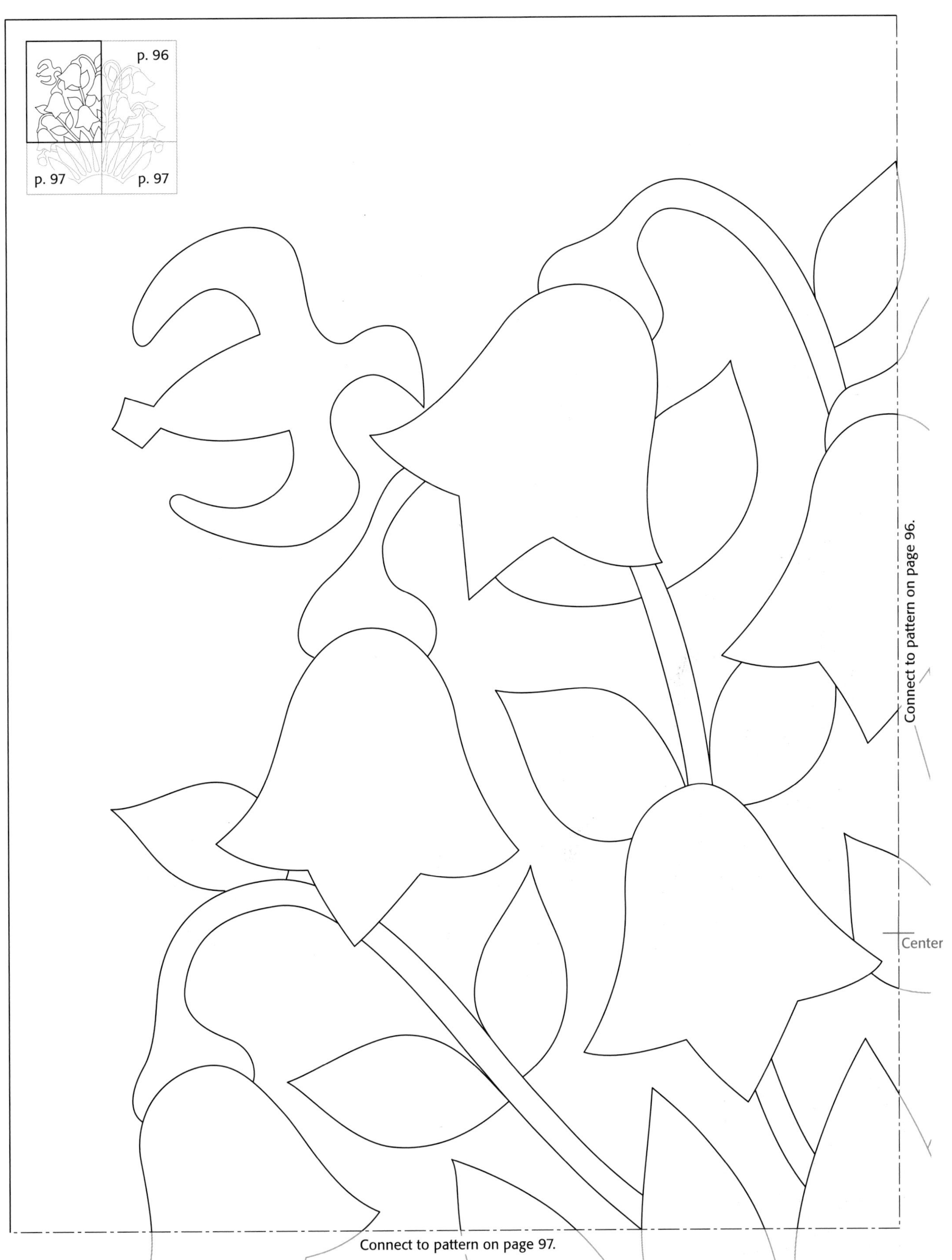
p. 96
p. 97
p. 97
Connect to pattern on page 96.
Center
Connect to pattern on page 97.

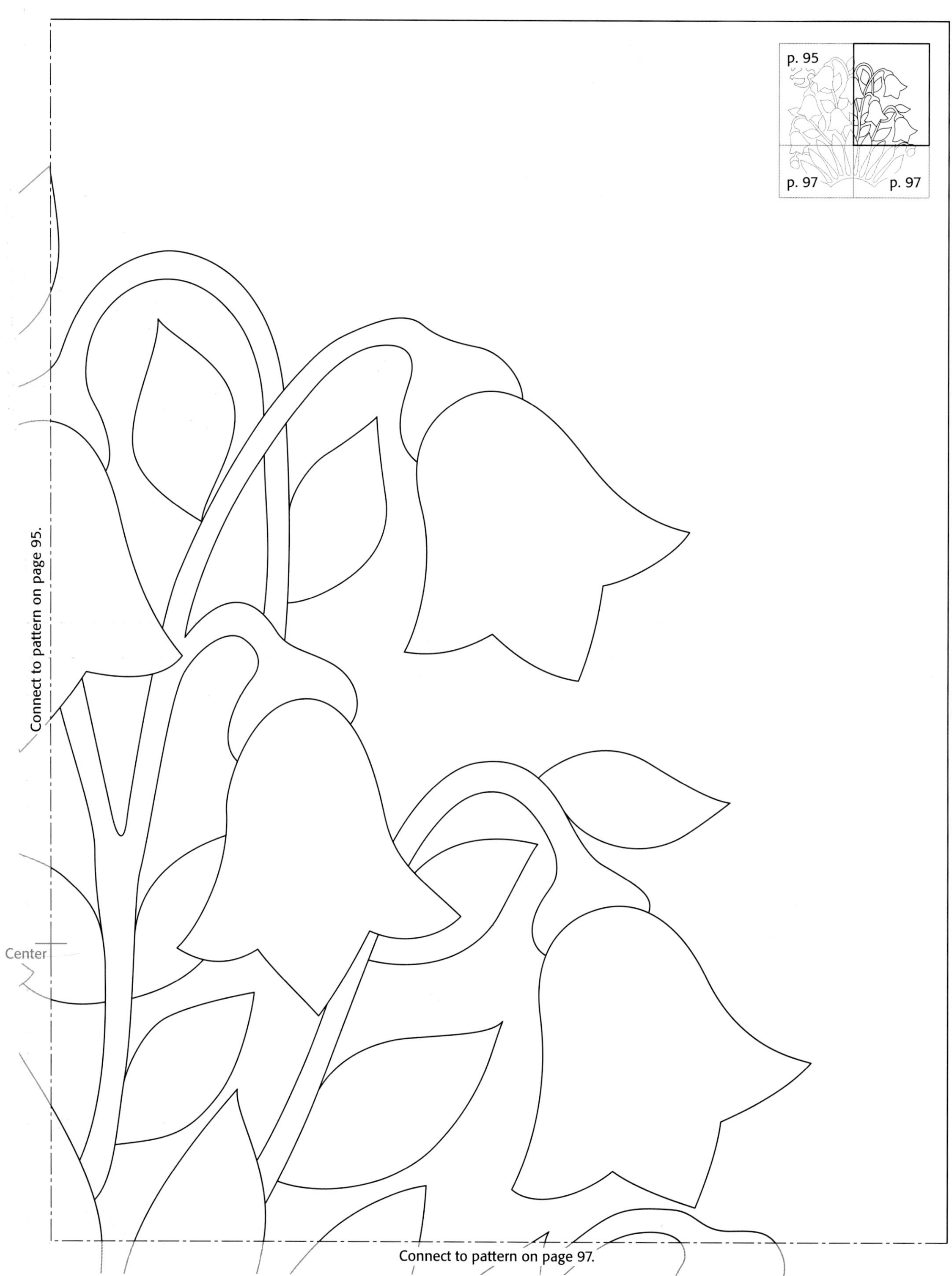
p. 95
p. 97
p. 97
Connect to pattern on page 95.
Center
Connect to pattern on page 97.

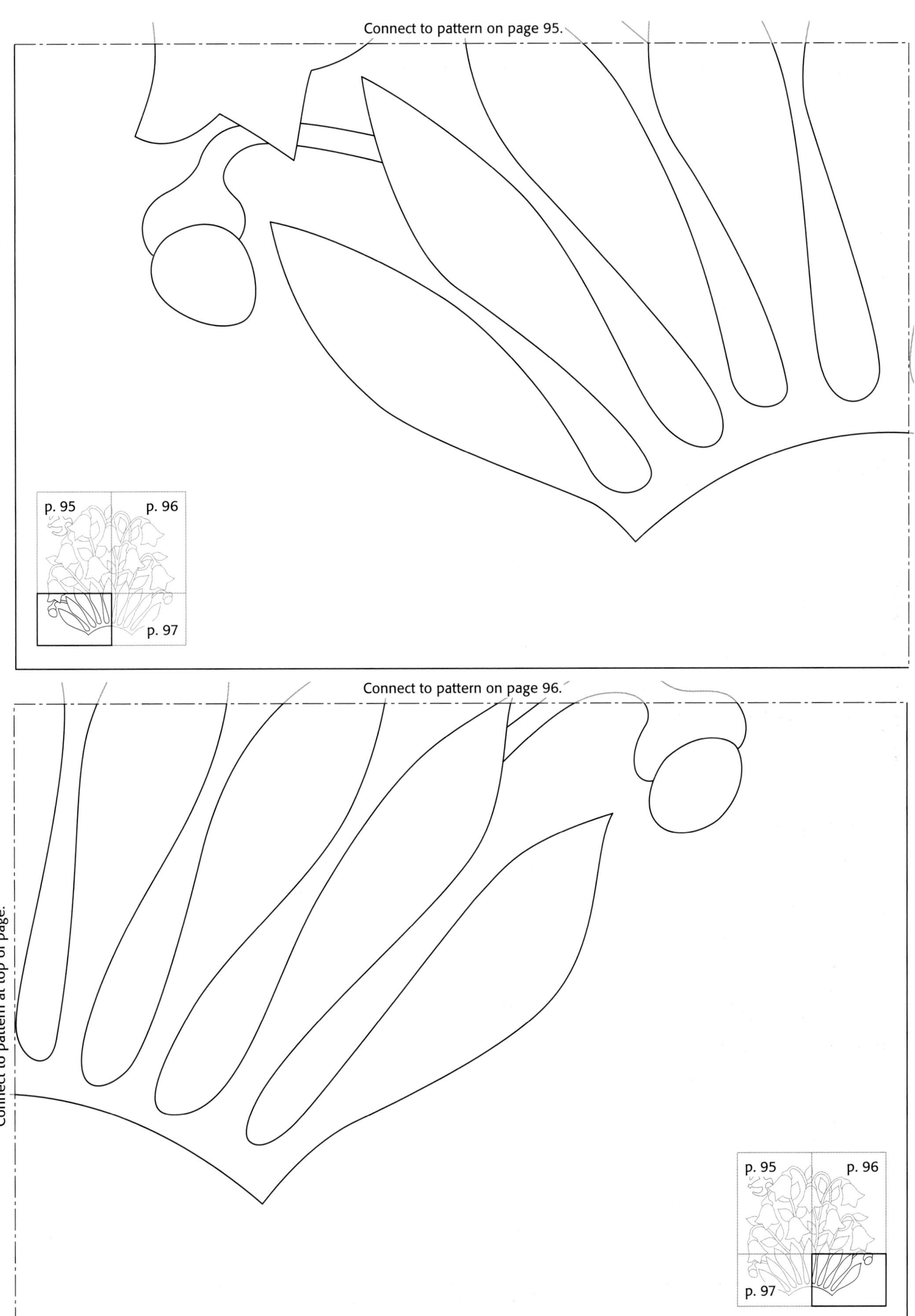
Connect to pattern on page 95.
Connect to pattern at bottom of page.
p. 95
p. 96
p. 97
Connect to pattern on page 96.
Connect to pattern at top of page.
p. 95
p. 96
p. 97

Carnations and Tulips

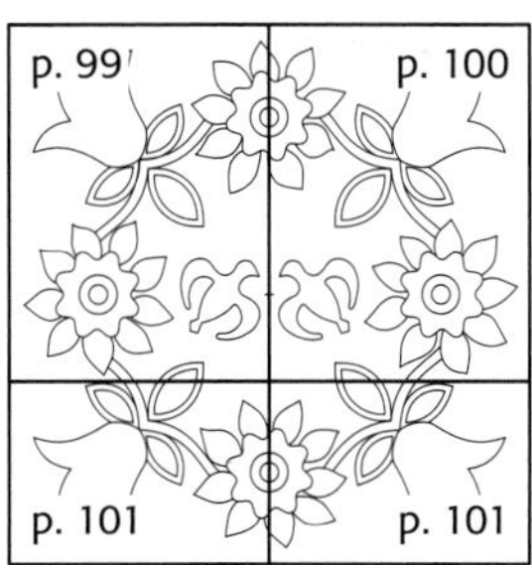

p. 100
p. 101
p. 101
Connect to pattern on page 100.
Center
Connect to pattern on page 101.

p. 99
p. 101
p. 101
Connect to pattern on page 99.
Center
Connect to pattern on page 101.

Connect to pattern on page 99.
Connect to pattern at bottom of page.
p. 99
p. 100
p. 101
Connect to pattern on page 100.
Connect to pattern at top of page.
p. 99
p. 100
p. 101

Asymmetrical Blooms and Buds

p. 103
p. 104
p. 105
p. 105

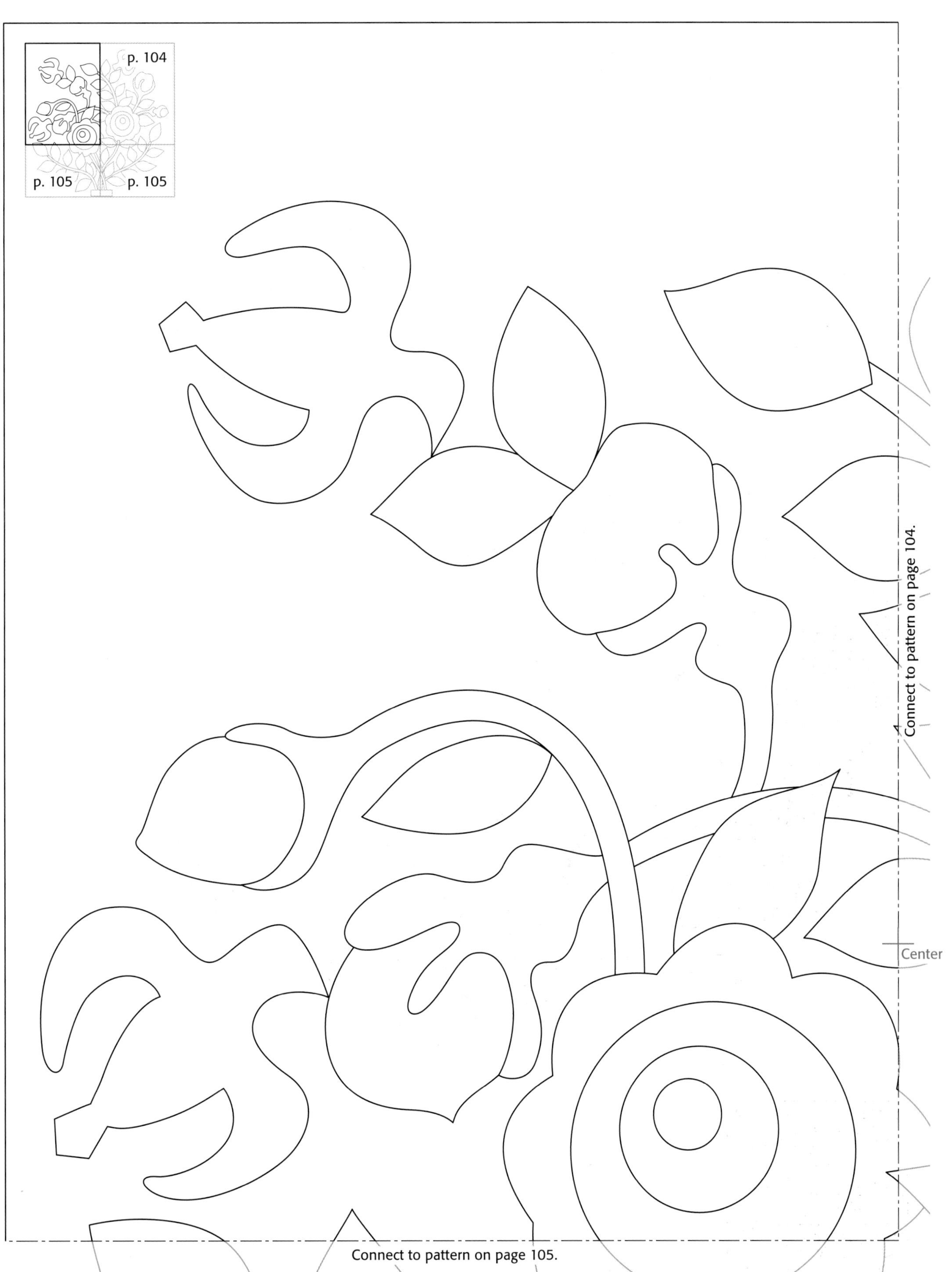
p. 104
p. 105
p. 105
Connect to pattern on page 104.
Center
Connect to pattern on page 105.

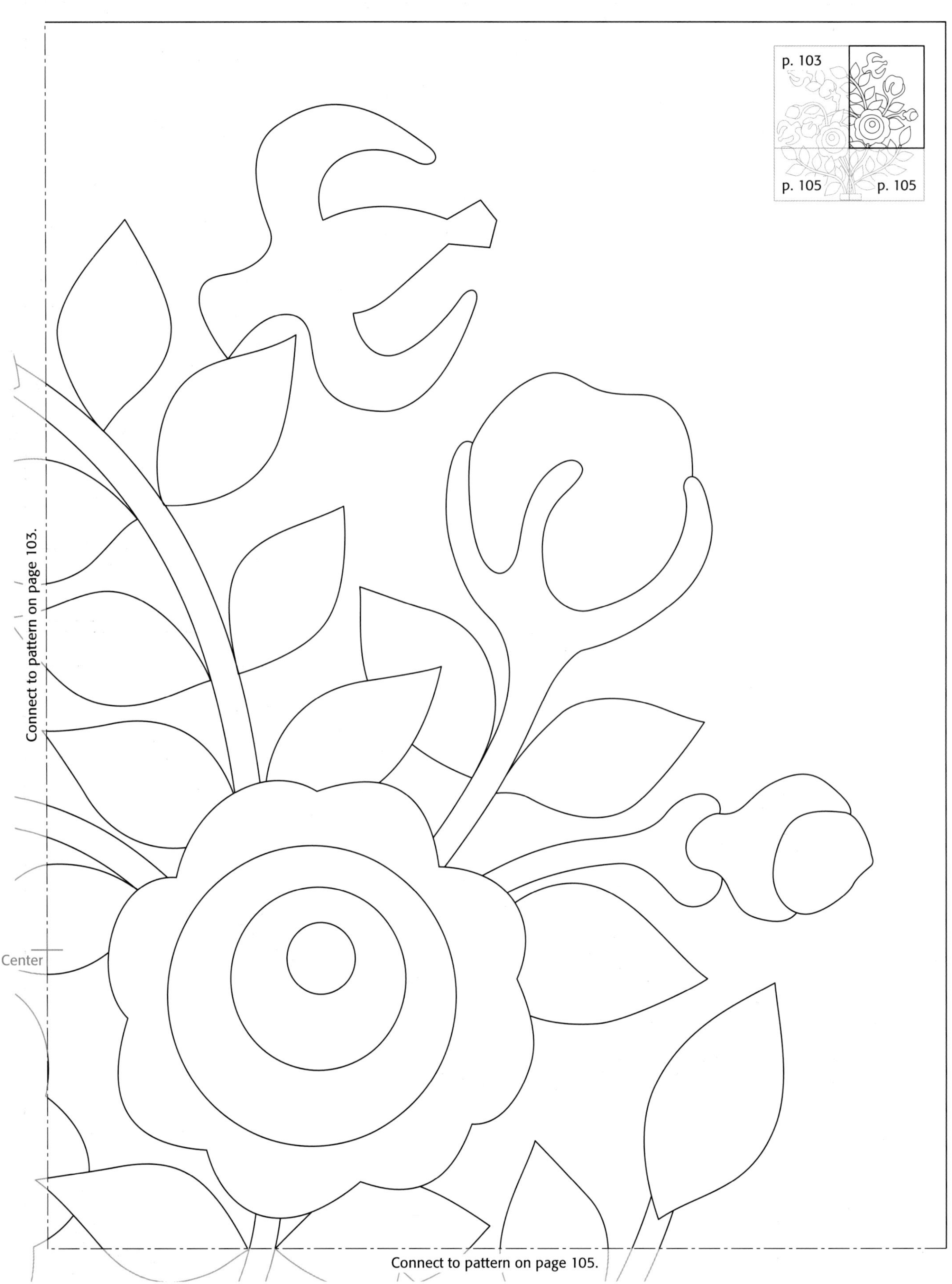
p. 103
p. 105
p. 105
Connect to pattern on page 103.
Center
Connect to pattern on page 105.

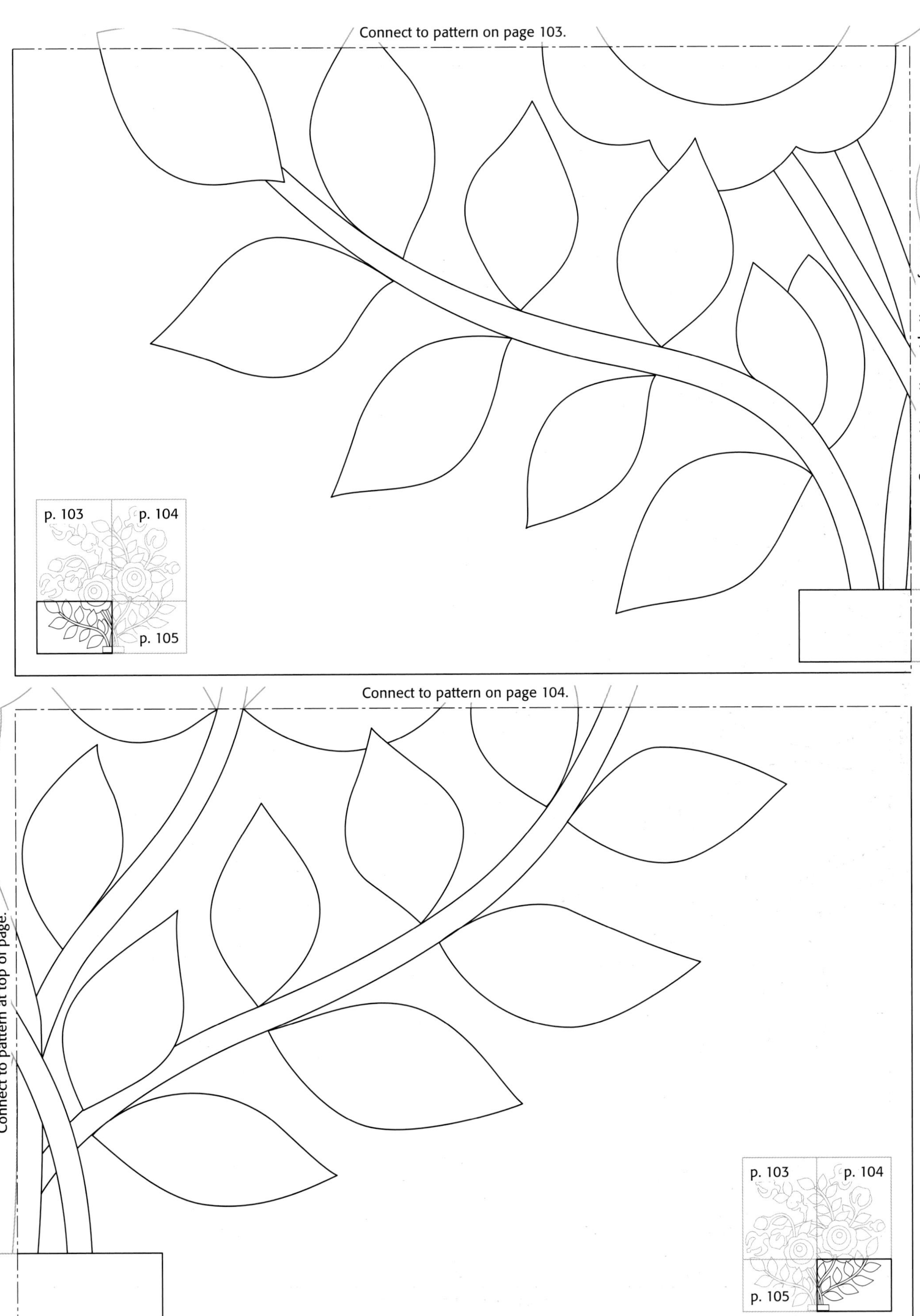
Connect to pattern on page 103.
Connect to pattern at bottom of page.
p. 103
p. 104
p. 105
Connect to pattern on page 104.
Connect to pattern at top of page.
p. 103
p. 104
p. 105

Peacocks in a Tree

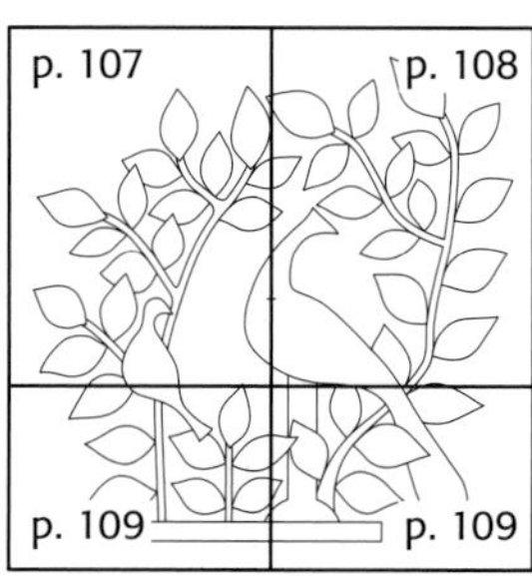

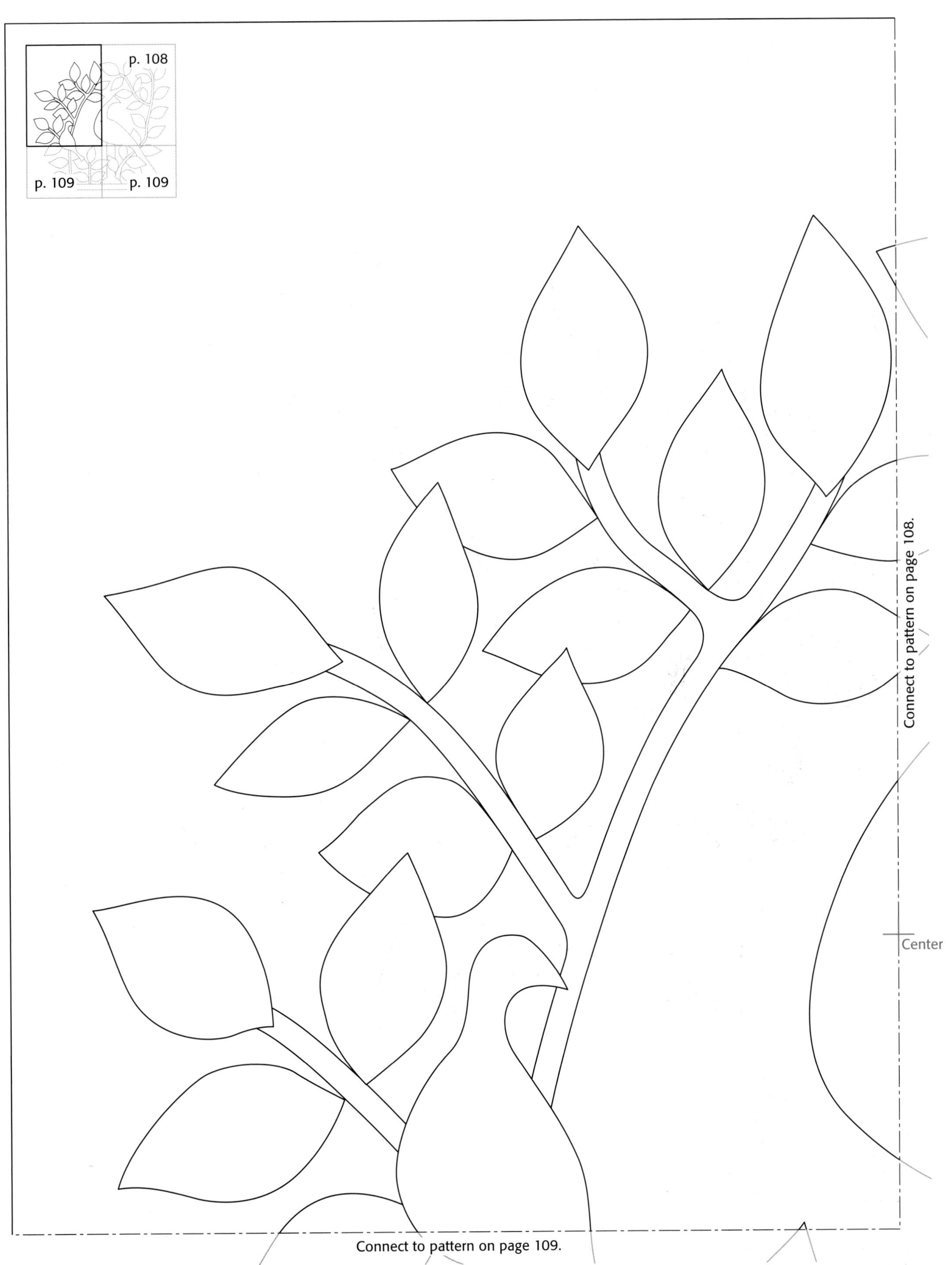
p. 108
p. 109
p. 109
Connect to pattern on page 108.
Center
Connect to pattern on page 109.

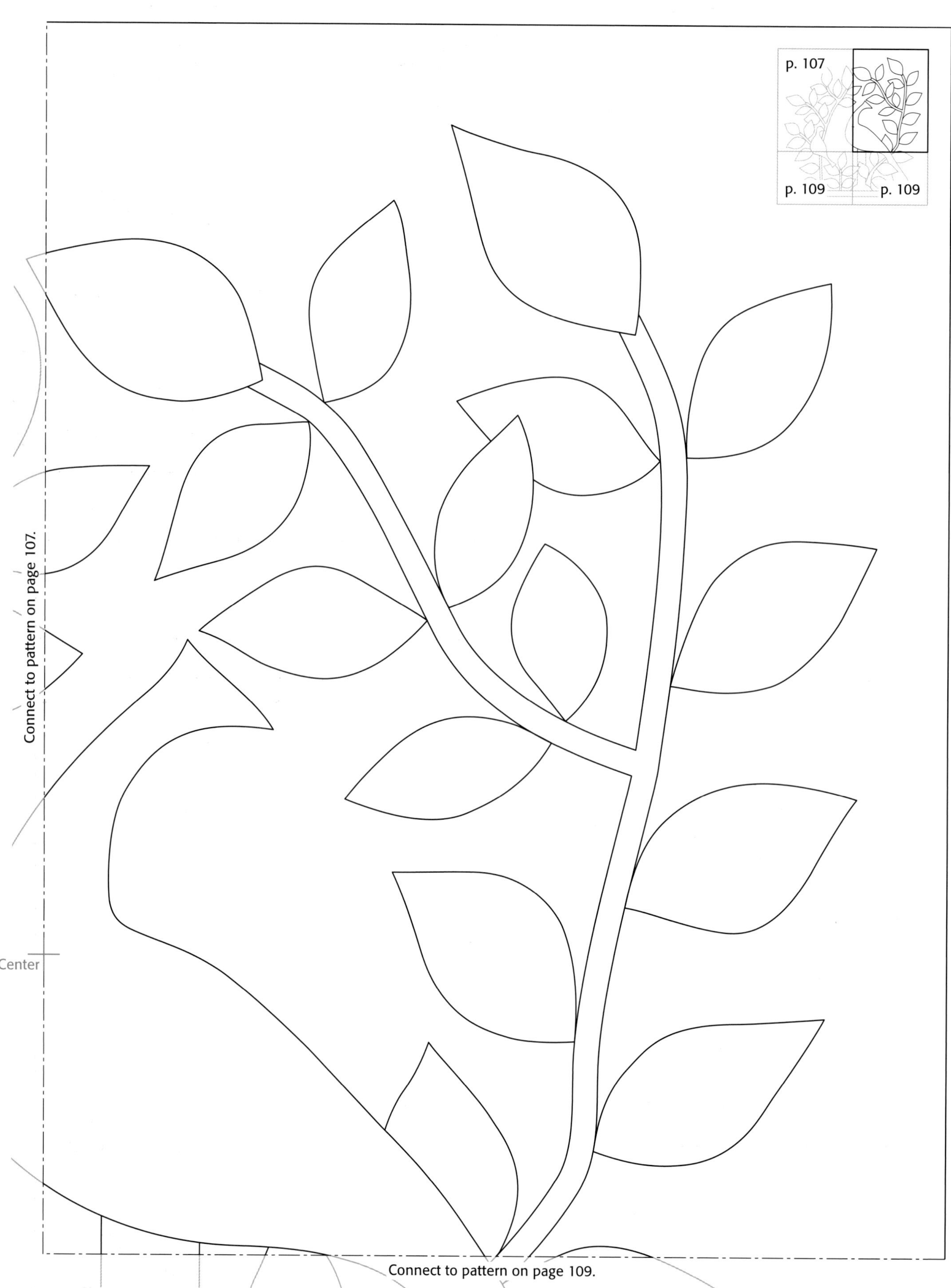
p. 107
p. 109
p. 109
Connect to pattern on page 107.
Center
Connect to pattern on page 109.

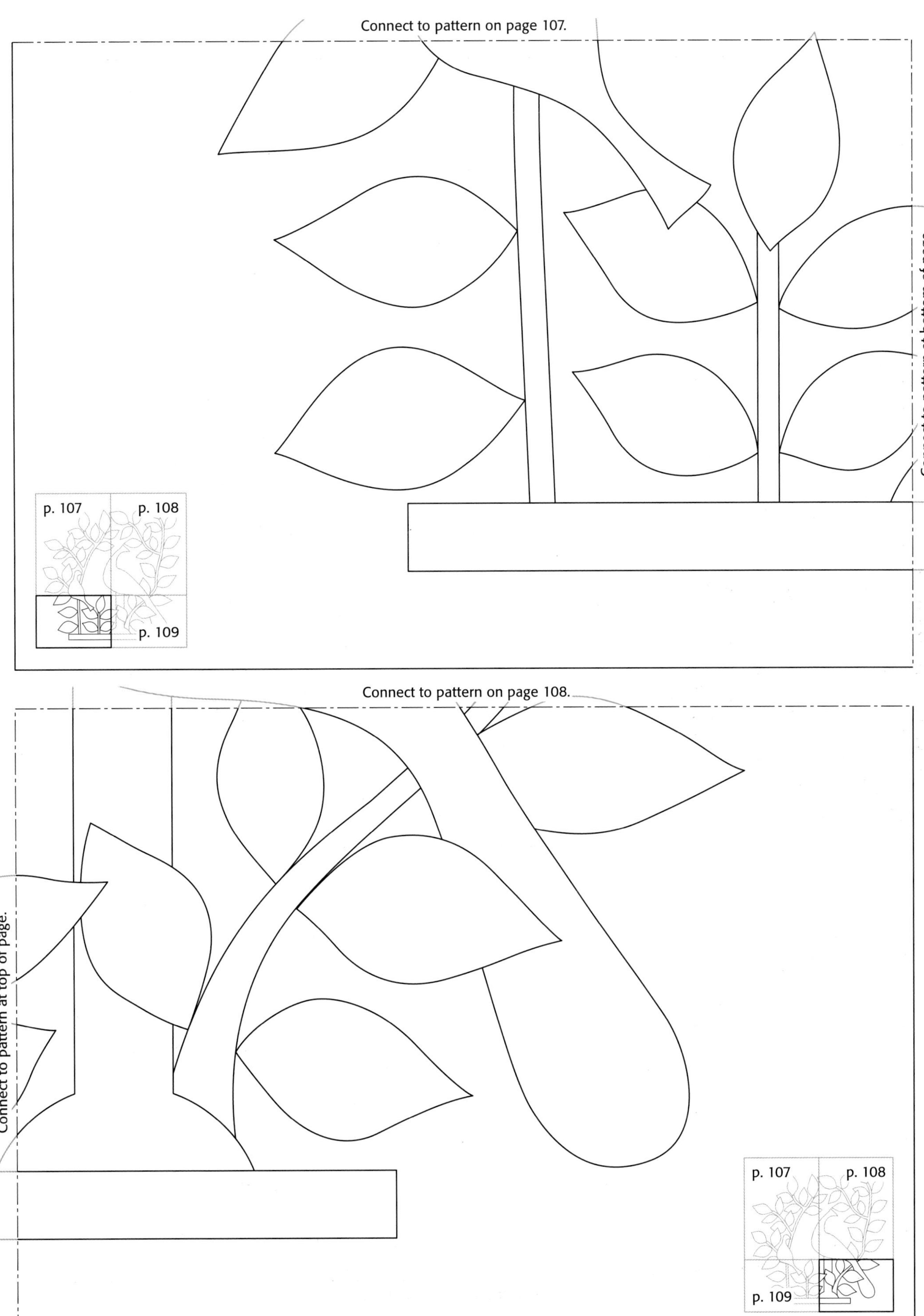
Connect to pattern on page 107.
Connect to pattern at bottom of page.
p. 107
p. 108
p. 109
Connect to pattern on page 108.
Connect to pattern at top of page.
p. 107
p. 108
p. 109

Lyre Wreath

p. 111 p. 112
p. 113 p. 113

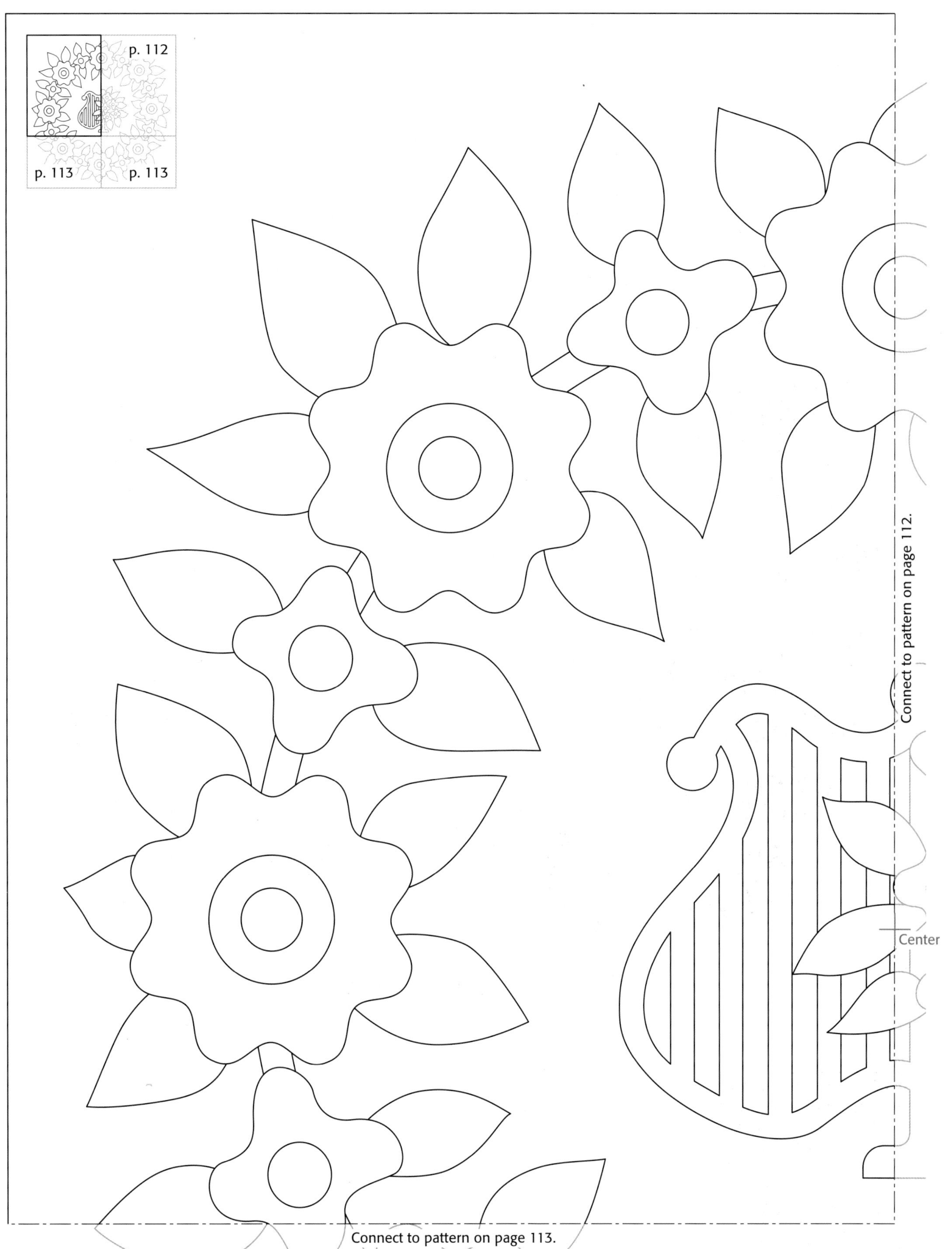
p. 112
p. 113
p. 113
Connect to pattern on page 112.
Center
Connect to pattern on page 113.

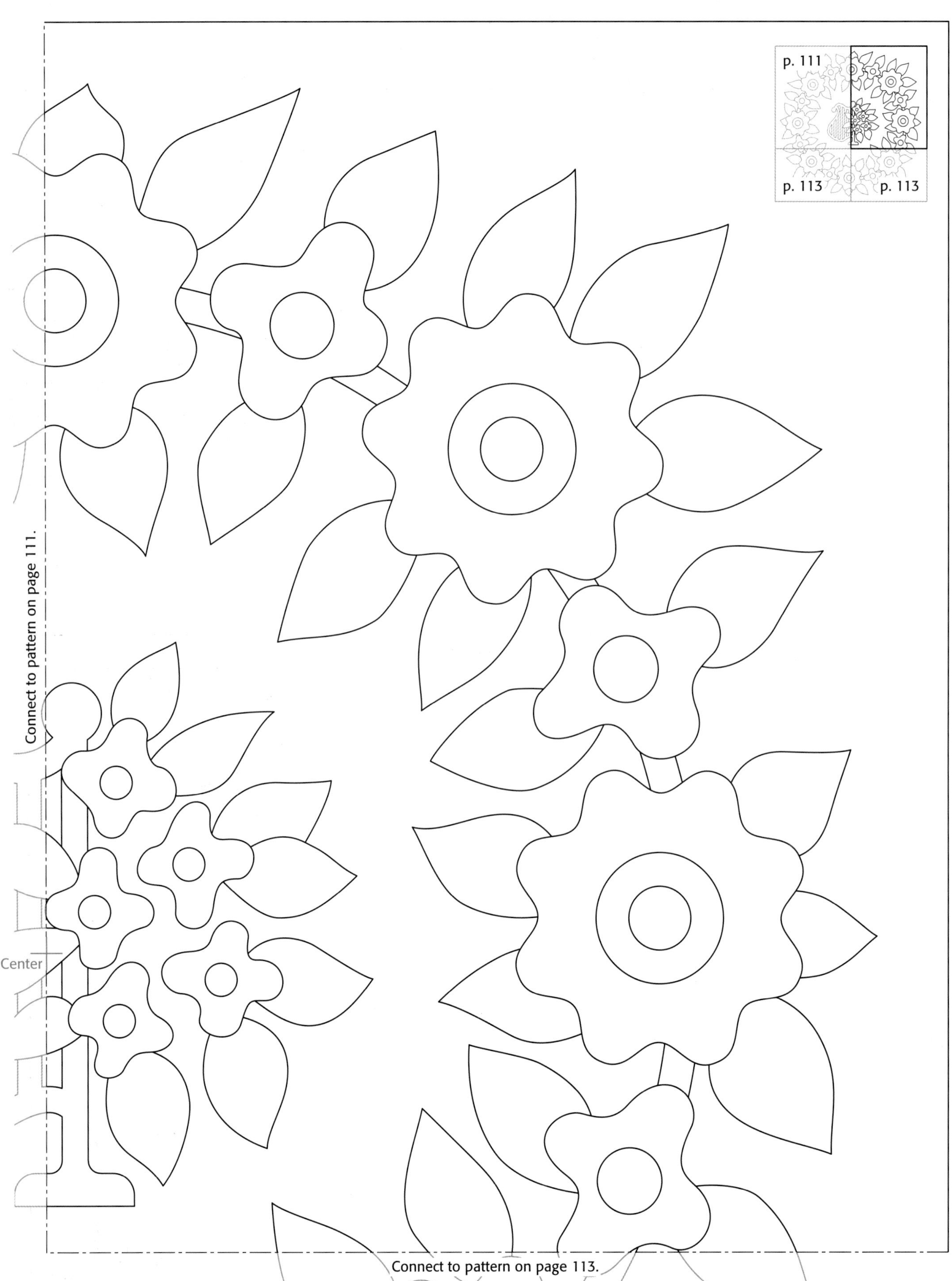
p. 111
p. 113
p. 113
Connect to pattern on page 111.
Center
Connect to pattern on page 113.

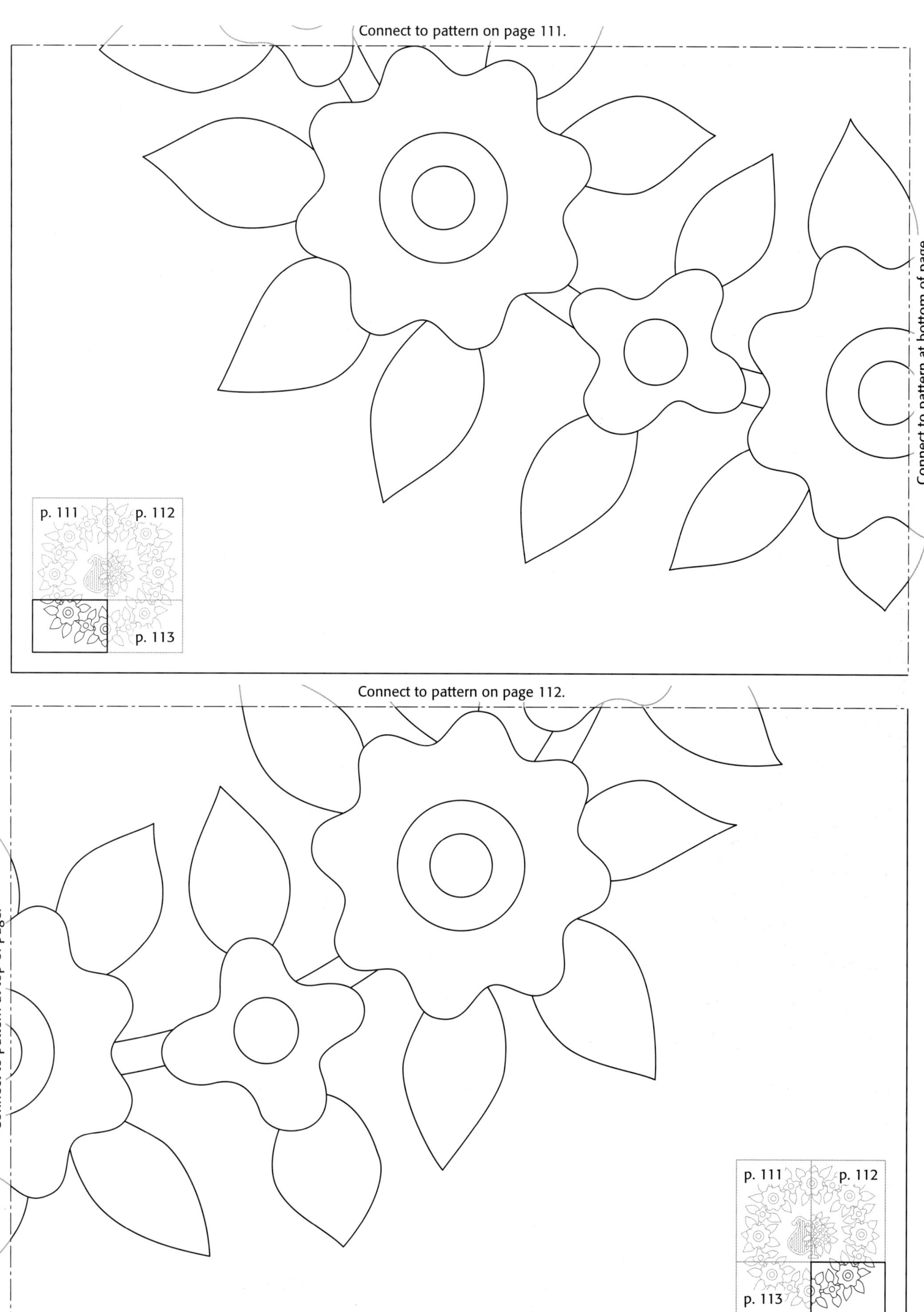
Connect to pattern on page 111.
Connect to pattern at bottom of page.
p. 111
p. 112
p. 113
Connect to pattern on page 112.
Connect to pattern at top of page.
p. 111
p. 112
p. 113

Border Appliqués for "Way Beyond Baltimore!"

Border Appliqués for "Pennsylvania Flower Garden"

p. 115
p. 117
p. 118
Begin side border pattern along this line.
Connect to pattern on page 115.
Border center
Connect to pattern on page 117.
Begin side border pattern along this line.

p. 115
p. 116
p. 118
Connect to pattern on page 116.
Border center
Connect to pattern on page 118.
Center of border pattern repeat

p. 115
p. 116
p. 117
Connect to pattern on page 117.
Border center
Begin border pattern repeat along this line.

Border Appliqués for "Rhapsody in Red and Black"

Center

Rotate pattern 180° around center.

Center

Connect to pattern on page 121.

Center
Connect to pattern on page 120.
p. 120

Center

Connect to pattern on page 123.

Center

Connect to pattern on page 122.

Center

Rotate pattern 180° around center.

RESOURCES

Benartex, Incorporated
1064 Memorial Highway
Oley, Pennsylvania 19547
610-987-0020
Quilt shops: Contact Benartex, Inc. for wholesale information on the fabrics used in the "Pennsylvania Flower Garden" quilt on page 48.

Big Board Enterprises
PO Box 748
Hughesville, MD 20637
800-441-6581
www.marshasbigboard.com

Jeanna Kimball's Foxglove Cottage
PO Box 698
Santa Clara, UT 84765
435-656-2071
FoxgloveCottage@worldnet.att.net
Size #11 Straw needles

Ladyfingers Sewing Studio
Authorized Bernina Sales and Service
800 Limekiln Rd.
Limekiln, PA 19535
610-689-0068
610-689-0067 fax
Fabric kits for the "Pennsylvania Flower Garden" quilt top shown on page 48
General sewing supplies
3 ½" serrated embroidery scissors
CAT paper

Mickey Lawler's Skydyes
PO Box 370116
West Hartford, CT 06137-0116
860-236-9117 fax
Skydyes@aol.com
www.skydyes.com
Hand-painted cottons and silks, fabric paints

Mulberry Silk & Things
(formerly dba Hapco Products)
210 Central
Rocheport, MO 65279
800-854-2726
573-698-2102
mulberrysilk@juno.com
www.mulberrysilk.com
Size #12 Sharps

Teresa M. Fusco
3804 Hill Top Ave.
Reading, PA 19605
tmfusco@berkscounty.com
Professional machine quilting

YLI Corporation
161 West Main St.
Rock Hill, SC 29730
800-296-8139
803-985-3100
803-985-3106 fax
www.ylicorp.com
100% silk threads (catalog $1.00)

BIBLIOGRAPHY

Hassel, Carla J. *Super Quilter II: Challenges for the Advanced Quilter.* Radnor, Pa.: Wallace-Homestead, 1982. Out of print.

Noble, Maurine. *Machine Quilting Made Easy.* Bothell, Wash.: That Patchwork Place, 1994.

Pearson, Nancy. *Floral Appliqué.* Saddle Brook, N.J.: Quilt House Publishing, 1994.

Safford, Carlton, and Robert Bishop. *America's Quilts and Coverlets.* New York: Weathervane Press, 1974. Out of print.

ABOUT THE AUTHOR

Photo by John Hamel

JANE TOWNSWICK is an accomplished author, editor, quilter, teacher, and former quilt-shop owner who has developed amazing expertise in hand appliqué. She has been featured as a guest artist and instructor at Elly Sienkiewicz's esteemed Appliqué Academy, and her work has been featured in *Quilter's Newsletter Magazine* and *American Quilter Magazine.* She is the author of *Artful Appliqué: The Easy Way*, published by Martingale & Company. Jane lives, teaches, and quilts in Allentown, Pennsylvania.